ENERGY CONSERVATION

with
Adhesives and Sealants

ENERGY
CONSERVATION
with
Adhesives and Sealants

By Robert S. Miller

Franklin International

2020 Bruck Street   P.O. Box 07802   Columbus, Ohio 43207

Manufactured in the United States of America

Text prepared and book designed by Scharff Associates, Ltd.

Current Printing (last digit)   10 9 8 7 6 5 4 3 2 1

ALSO BY ROBERT S. MILLER
Home Construction Projects with Adhesives and Glues

Acknowledgments

The author is deeply indebted to many individuals who helped in many ways to create this book. Without a doubt, the Elastomers Laboratory section of Franklin International under the direction of George Butts and Denny Doyle have, through the years, provided the writer with much guidance and insight into both the technical and practical use and application of adhesives.

There are many others both inside Franklin International as well as outside the company to whom we owe a great deal of gratitude for their direct and indirect contributions in bringing this book to fruition. Our thanks goes out to all for their help, guidance, and patience.

We would like to thank the following companies for providing photographs and other resource information: Owens-Corning Fiberglas Corp., W. R. Grace & Co., the Dow Chemical Company, Manville Building Materials Corporation, and the Homasote Company.

Library of Congress Cataloging in Publication Data

Miller, Robert S.
  Energy conservation with adhesives and sealants.

  Includes index.
    1. Dwellings—Energy conservation.   2. Dwellings—
Insulation.   3. Adhesives.   4. Sealing compounds.
I. Title.
TJ163.5.D86M55   1986   644   85-27505
ISBN 0-937558-13-3

Contents

Preface		iv
1.	Conservation and Comfort	1
2.	Understanding Energy Efficiency	7
3.	Making a Home Energy Audit	23
4.	Adhesives and Weatherizing	31
5.	Types of Caulks and Sealants	45
6.	Sealing Your House with Caulks	59
7.	Weatherstripping Materials	71
8.	Weatherstripping Windows and Doors	79
9.	Choosing and Buying Insulation	91
10.	Insulating Attics and Ceilings	103
11.	Insulating Walls	119
12.	Insulating Foundations	135
13.	Insulating Steel Buildings	145
14.	Other Energy-Saving Techniques	151
	Glossary	161
	Index	169

Preface

Being a leader in the manufacturing of adhesives and sealants, Franklin International saw a need to more thoroughly inform the consumer about the various types available and their uses in home energy conservation projects.

This book covers a wide range of subjects to prepare the amateur do-it-yourselfer for choosing from among the many types of adhesives, sealants, and weatherstripping and insulating materials that are available, estimating home insulating and sealing requirements, and actually purchasing and installing the energy-saving materials.

The subjects of caulking and weatherstripping are dealt with in detail, while the importance of good ventilation is also emphasized and explained. Subjects also covered are the installation of wall, floor, attic, foundation, and ceiling insulation, with both general purpose adhesives and specialty adhesive products, in specific weatherizing jobs. An extensive glossary aids in the understanding of technical terms.

I have known the author of this book, Robert S. Miller, for 20 of his 33 years in the adhesives industry. He has worked in both the industrial and consumer fields of adhesive and sealant applications. Having been with Franklin International for the past 20 years, Bob has served as marketing manager of our Consumer Products Division and is presently general manager of this division. He holds a B.S. degree in marketing from the Ohio State University, has done graduate work at Syracuse University, and recently received his M.B.A. from Ohio University. As with his first book *Home Construction Projects with Adhesives and Glues,* I feel that the author's wide experience in the construction as well as the adhesives and sealants industry qualifies him from a practical standpoint to write in a layman's language about actual home applications of adhesives and sealants.

It is our sincere hope that this book will enable the reader to undertake nearly any sort of weatherizing operation—and do it with confidence and knowledge.

L. Thomas Williams, Jr.
Chairman of the Board and Chief Executive Officer
Franklin International

Conservation and Comfort 1

One of the elemental needs of man is shelter. From tents of goat hair and thatch-roofed mud huts to the suburban split-level homes of today, shelters have been designed to provide man with warmth in winter, relief from summer heat, a refuge from the elements, and protection from danger. In short, shelters have kept man comfortable and safe.

While the primary function of a modern home is still comfort, an estimated 40 million homes across the country are not adequately protected from the weather. Yours may be one of them. An energy audit (as explained in detail in Chapter 3) will help you pinpoint what areas need to be weatherproofed. By taking corrective steps, such as filling living spaces with insulation, filling cracks with caulking, sealing windows and doors with weatherstripping, repairing or replacing ill-fitting doors, and eliminating energy-wasting habits and appliances, you can reduce your energy consumption by 30% to 60%, cut back on your fuel bills, and live more comfortably.

Many people mistakenly equate conserving energy with turning the thermostat down to 58°, wearing bulky clothes around the house, and taking cold showers. This picture of energy conservation is very misleading; saving energy does not have to mean sacrificing comfort or convenience.

The Use of Adhesives and Sealants

The task of weatherproofing your home can be made easier by the use of good adhesives and sealants. Mortars, mastics, sealants, and cements have long been used to build homes and to make them impervious to the elements. Many types of construction adhesives can be used to hold insulating materials in place, and they are particularly helpful in most weatherizing projects.

Adhesives have several advantages over other fastening methods: They bond over entire surfaces, providing a uniform distribution of stress; they bond to materials that cannot be penetrated by nails, and enable you to fasten materials in tight spots and small areas where nailing is difficult or impossible; they hold up well under moist conditions and are rustproof; they reduce thermal and acoustical transmission; and they are considered faster and easier to use by most inexperienced do-it-yourselfers. By using adhesives, you also avoid puncturing the fastened material, an inevitable result of nailing that can cause considerable energy loss.

In addition to providing a basic knowledge of the various insulating materials, adhesives, and sealants that are available to make your home energy efficient,

1

this book will also explain how to "do it yourself." You will learn how to insulate attics, ceilings, roofs, walls, and foundations; fill cracks and openings with caulks and sealants; and weatherstrip windows and doors. However, before getting into the actual process of weatherizing your home, it is a good idea first to explain the factors that create a comfortable environment and how weather-proofing with the aid of adhesives and sealants can increase comfort.

Comfort Factors

Four environmental factors are crucial for human comfort: temperature, rela-tive humidity, air velocity, and the temperature of surrounding surfaces (known as the mean radiant temperature). By recognizing the importance of these factors, and understanding how they interact, we can find ways to conserve energy while maintaining comfort.

The proper combination of temperature and humidity plays a large role in human comfort (Fig. 1-1). At a given temperature, people feel warmer as the relative humidity increases. In winter, a higher relative humidity can make the indoor environment feel warmer, too. On the other hand, as relative humidity is reduced, higher temperatures are needed to maintain the same feeling of warmth. Thus, by manipulating temperature and/or humidity, you can increase comfort, and weatherproofing will enable you to maintain a level of comfort at a lower thermostat setting due to the reduction of cold, dry air entering the house.

15% HUMIDITY 75°

45% HUMIDITY 75°

90% HUMIDITY 75°

Fig. 1-1: Relative humidity has a profound effect on comfort.

Fuel bills can be reduced up to 2% to 3% for each degree that a thermostat setting is reduced. Suggested ideal energy-saving thermostat settings are 65°F during the day and 55°F at night. A house that will be empty for several days can easily be kept at 45°F without fear of frozen water pipes.

Table 1-1 gives comparisons of room temperatures and mean radiant temperatures that provide equal comfort.

Table 1-1: The Comfort Range of Mean Radiant Temperature and Air Temperature

Mean radiant temperature	65	66	67	68	69	70	71	72	73	74	75	76	77	78	79	80
Air temperature	77	75.6	74.2	72.8	71.4	70	68.6	67.2	65.8	64.4	63	61.6	60.2	58.8	57.4	56

Controlling humidity is also important because high moisture levels in a home can cause condensation. Caution is advised when adding moisture to indoor air. Moist air seeps into walls and attics, where, it condenses and causes structural decay. For this reason you should "tighten up" the inside of your home by caulking and sealing air leaks. Besides reducing heat loss and air infiltration, you have added the benefit of protecting your home from moisture damage.

Drafts are annoying sources of discomfort that are easily corrected. There are two sources of drafts: cold air seeping into the house through cracks and openings and convective air currents inside the house (Fig. 1-2). Filling air passageways with caulks and sealants will eliminate the drafts caused by infiltration. Convective air currents caused by warm air coming in contact with cold surfaces can be reduced by insulating walls and windows.

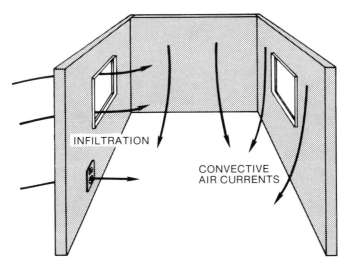

INFILTRATION

CONVECTIVE AIR CURRENTS

Fig. 1-2: Infiltrating and convective air currents create uncomfortable drafts.

Another factor affecting comfort is the temperature of the surrounding surfaces, also known as the mean radiant temperature (Fig. 1-3). Since heat always radiates from warmer matter to cooler matter—from people to the cooler surfaces around them—raising the mean radiant temperature creates more comfortable conditions.

You can create a higher mean radiant temperature by insulating walls, floors, ceilings, and windows. Passive solar homes are frequently cited as being more comfortable than conventional homes because of their highly insulated shells and the presence of massive walls and floors that radiate stored heat.

Another way to increase comfort is to reflect the body's radiant heat loss back into the room. The foil backing found on some insulation acts as a radiant energy reflector. Energy rays bounce off the foil and are deflected back into the living space.

COMFORTABLE   UNCOMFORTABLE

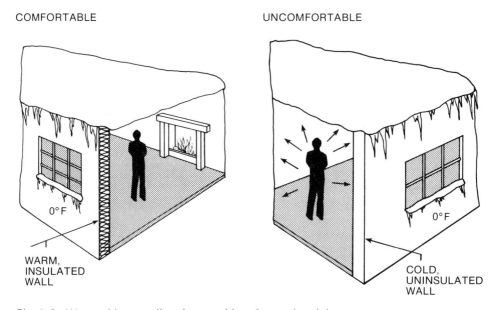

Fig. 1-3: Warm objects radiate heat; cold surfaces absorb heat.

History of Adhesives and Sealants As Energy Savers

No one knows when adhesives and sealants were first used. Their use as energy savers and fasteners—to make homes more liveable and comfortable—goes back further than written history, and the experts can only speculate on which was developed first—the nail or an adhesive. We do know that the ancient Babylonians used a bituminous pitch to cement ivory eyeballs in their statuary. This same pitch was used as a construction material in the ancient account of Noah's ark. Egyptian furniture assembled with a glue made from boiled animal parts is still strongly bonded after 3,000 years. The Assyrians used a clay mortar to hold their brick buildings together, and the Romans developed a hydraulic limestone mortar that was used in building their great cities and aqueducts.

The technological explosion that accompanied the Renaissance brought about the development of many new adhesives. The colonists brought new adhesives and sealants to the New World. Animal glues were made from animal parts boiled down to a jelly. This dried mass was pounded into powder, mixed with water, and heated to make an excellent furniture glue. Until the twentieth century, this was the most widely used adhesive and is still used today.

The colonists also brought with them sealants made of plant resins such as pine sap. These were used to waterproof and preserve ships and other marine installations. They also developed mortars from clay and lime to seal their log cabins.

The development of petroleum byproducts, plastics, and synthetic rubber began to revolutionize the adhesive and sealant industry in the 1950s. Today adhesives and sealants are formulated to withstand extremes of temperature, tension, compression, and moisture to last for decades, thus making them very suitable for home construction, repair, and renovation. But despite the constant modifications and improvements, the link to the past has not been completely severed. Clay is still used as filler material to strengthen even high-performance sealants. Oil-based caulks are still 60% to 75% clay. Coal tars are still used in roofing cements and asphalt sealers.

The greatest number of developments has come in the adhesive industry. Epoxies, acrylics, SBR rubber, latex, neoprenes, polyesters, polyvinyl acetates, phenolics, and cyanoacrylates are just a few examples of the many new adhesives on the market today. The construction industry has been quick to utilize these new adhesives; in fact, no other method of attachment would be satisfactory for many applications. Adhesives are used to install subfloors (Fig. 1-4), sheathing, drywall, paneling, floor tiles, ceiling tiles, roofing materials, and concrete. They can even bond metal to metal in nonstructural joints.

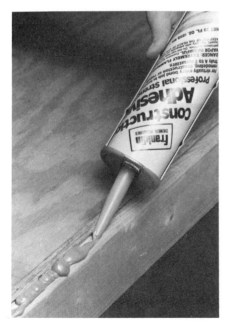

Fig. 1-4: The modern multi-purpose construction adhesive—shown here being used to install a subfloor—is a versatile, general mastic designed for a wide range of construction applications; it is virtually the only adhesive you will ever need for most bonding jobs in the home.

When performing home remodeling, renovations, and additions, it is wise to take advantage of the opportunity to improve the home's energy efficiency. Remodeling often exposes the studding in walls, and you should use this opportunity to add in-wall fiberglass insulation. If you are converting your basement into a living area or rec room, you should remember to install rigid board insulation or some other type of insulation as part of the overall project. To put it simply: don't miss any convenient opportunity to weatherize. By following the directions and illustrations in this book, and by using quality adhesives and sealants, you can see for yourself how easy it is to make your home both comfortable and energy efficient.

The Financial Overview of Energy Saving

Unfortunately, there is no such thing as an "average" American house when it comes to energy losses. HUD's recently released figures on heating losses in a typical uninsulated frame house show that 30% to 35% of all heat loss occurs through the ceiling; 25% to 30% through the floors; 15% to 20% through the walls; 10% to 15% through infiltration; 10% to 15% through doors and windows; and about 2% through the ductwork.

Table 1-2 will serve as a guideline as you plan your energy conserving improvements. The table is based on a 1400 square foot uninsulated ranch house that was upgraded to R-19 in the ceiling and R-11 in the floors.

Table 1-2: Typical Weatherizing Saving Per Year		
Improvement	Cost*	Dollar Saving/Year	% Fuel Bill Saving/Year
Attic (Ceiling) Insulation	$300-$450	$125-$400	10%-25%
Floor Insulation	$300-$450	$60-$110	5%-6%
Wall Insulation	$500-$1200	$95-$160	4%-8%
Ductwork Insulation	$20-$60	$10-$30	1%-2%
Water Heater Insulation	$20-$30	$5-$20	1%-2%
Storm Windows and Doors	$175-$800	$50-$300	6%-10%
Weatherstripping	$25-$100	$10-$500	1%-4%
Caulking	$20-$75	$10-$40	2%-4%
Totals	$1360-$3165	$365-$1560	30%-60%

*Improvement costs here include only materials, not labor.

Understanding Energy Efficiency 2

Analyzing your home's energy efficiency can be a very bewildering task. A house is subject to the weather of the geographic region in which it is located; but each house also is subject to the microclimatic factors, such as nearby trees, buildings, hills, bodies of water, which can all affect the exposure of a house to sun and wind, which influence the flow of heat through the house. Also, the more a house is insulated, the less effective additional weatherproofing will be in further reducing energy costs. For example, an uninsulated, drafty house may be losing 45% of its total heat through the ceiling and attic. Adding 6" fiberglass batt insulation to the attic floor may reduce the cost of heating this house by 30% to 40%. On the other hand, the heat lost through the ceiling and attic of a well-insulated house may account for only 15% of its total heating costs. In this case, placing an additional 6" of fiberglass insulation in the attic will cost as much as in the first example, but the energy saving may be only 10% of the total cost of heating. For this homeowner, it may be wiser to thoroughly caulk and weatherstrip to prevent air infiltration, the major cause of heat loss in well-insulated houses.

But before analyzing your home's energy efficiency, you should understand some basic principles of heat energy and energy conservation. This chapter will explain what heat is, how it travels, and how you can measure heat loss and heat gain in your house. This information will equip you to make "expert" choices of weatherproofing techniques that will save energy.

UNDERSTANDING HEAT FLOW

Heat is a form of energy associated with the random motion of molecules in gaseous, liquid, and solid matter. Molecules even in seemingly rigid, solid objects are in constant, random motion, and the motion of the molecules represents heat. The more *thermal energy* (heat) a substance or object contains, the greater is its amount of molecular movement or excitation.

It is important to distinguish heat and temperature. *Temperature* is the measure of *how* hot something is, or of the *level* of molecular excitation in an object. But a measurement of an object's *heat,* as such, is the measure of the total amount of heat energy, or molecular excitation, in the object. For example, the level of heat (temperature) of a tip of a burning match may be very high, but the match tip contains far less total heat energy than, say, a bucket of cold water. Another example is that of two buckets of water, one holding one gallon and the other holding ten gallons, both having a temperature of 50°F; the larger one contains ten times the heat of the smaller pail. Temperature is only a measurement of the concentration of heat in an object, but heat is the energy itself that can be conserved and put to work in your home.

Heat flow is actually the transfer of thermal energy. Heat flow occurs in three ways: *conduction, convection,* and *radiation*—all of which are involved in the heat gain and heat loss of a house. Heat always travels from an area of warm temperature (or a high concentration of heat) to an area of cool temperature (a low concentration of heat). As an example, think of a house with a constant temperature of 70°F. At a given outdoor temperature, say 40°F, the temperature difference is 30° and heat loss occurs at a certain rate. If the outdoor temperature drops to 10°F, the temperature difference doubles, causing the house to lose twice as much heat per hour. Note that the direction of heat flow is reversed for air-conditioned homes in the summer. Heat is transferred *into* the house, but at a slower rate due to a smaller temperature difference.

Transfer of Heat by Conduction

The primary mode of heat flow in a house is *conduction.* Conduction is the flow of heat through matter. When an object is exposed to temperatures higher than its own, the molecules at the surface of the object are heated. These molecules, in turn, pass this energy inside to cooler adjacent molecules. In this way, heat is dispersed through the object until all of its molecules reach a uniform temperature. An example of this is a metal pan on a hot stove (Fig. 2-1). Heat travels from the bottom of the pan out to the end of the handle, and the handle soon becomes hot to the touch.

Some materials conduct heat much more readily than others. Steel conducts heat 400 times faster than wood and 1,000 times faster than fiberglass insulation. Wood conducts heat slowly because it is composed of millions of air-filled cells. Gases are poor conductors, and materials filled with tiny air pockets are usually poor conductors. A good example of this is rigid urethane foam insulation. Urethane foam is composed of numerous, tiny, sealed air pockets and has a higher resistance to heat flow than any other building material.

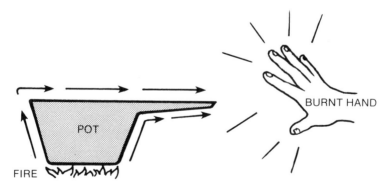

Fig. 2-1: Heat travels by conduction from the base of the pot to the end of the handle.

Every component in the structure of your house conducts heat. In summer, heat is absorbed from the warm air outside and conducted from component to component until it reaches the cool interior of your house. In winter, the direction of heat transfer reverses. Walls, ceilings, windows, doors, and floors absorb heat from the warm air in the house and conduct the heat through the frame and into the cold outside air and ground.

Transfer of Heat by Convection

Convection may be defined as the transfer of heat from one point to another by moving air, water, gas, or any other material that is not solid. For example, as cool molecules of a nonsolid substance such as the air in your house come into physical contact with a warm object such as a radiator, some of the heat at the surface of the warm object is transferred to the cooler, adjacent air molecules (Fig. 2-2). As the air warms, it expands, becomes less dense, and rises. As the warmer air molecules rise, they are replaced by cooler molecules that, in turn, are heated, and that also become less dense, and rise. This results in a continuous movement of the air and transfer of heat. When heat alone is responsible for the air current, the process is called *natural convection*. When cool air is mechanically forced across a warm surface, the heat transfer is called *forced convection*.

Convection is involved in heat loss in several ways. As warm air rises and comes in contact with a cool surface, such as an uninsulated wall or window, air molecules transfer heat to the cool surface, which in turn conducts the heat away from the interior. As the air loses heat, it becomes cool, more dense, and sinks. The cool, sinking air creates a downdraft of cool air at the floor. On a cold

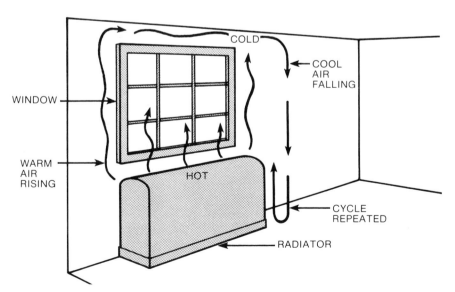

Fig. 2-2: As cool air warms, it rises. As warm air cools, it falls. As air is alternately warmed and cooled, convective air currents are created.

winter day, even in an otherwise warm room, these cold drafts can become uncomfortable and noticeable.

Convective heat loss also occurs when there are ceiling cracks that allow the rising air to seep into the attic where the warmth is transferred to the outdoors. This escape of warm air is sometimes called the stack, or chimney, effect (Fig. 2-3). Escaping warm air causes a drop in air pressure inside the house, and is known as *exfiltration*. That permits the greater air pressure on the outside to push cool air into the house. This process is known as *infiltration*. When exfiltration and infiltration occur simultaneously, warm air is replaced in a process of convection by cool air that must constantly be heated to a comfortable temperature.

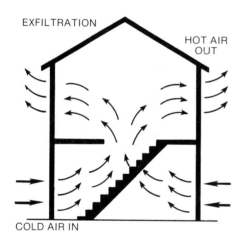

Fig. 2-3: Rising warm air escapes through cracks in the upper area of the house, drawing cool air into the house through openings in the lower parts of the building.

The wind is always a factor in infiltration and convective heat loss (Fig. 2-4). Wind, as it blows against a house, compresses air against the outer surfaces of walls, windows, doors, etc., and pushes the air through cracks in the structure. Then as the wind passes over and around the house, it produces a drop in pressure on the leeward side of the house. This drop in pressure draws air out of the other side of the house. Infiltration and exfiltration increase dramatically as wind velocity increases. A 30 mph wind will cause 15 times more infiltration and exfiltration than a 5 mph wind.

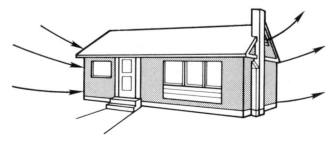

Fig. 2-4: The force of wind against the windward side of a house pushes air into the house, while the drop in air pressure on the leeward side pulls air out of the house.

Transfer of Heat by Radiation

A third way heat travels is by *radiation.* Radiation is the transfer of energy in the form of energy rays or waves. Unlike conduction or convection, this means of transfer is unaided by any conducting material and occurs in all directions simultaneously. All objects—people, houses, even rocks—radiate heat energy, but the best example is the sun (Fig. 2-5). The sun showers our solar system with many types of energy waves, some of which are absorbed and stored as thermal energy or heat.

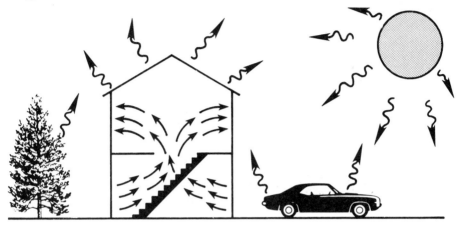

Fig. 2-5: All objects radiate heat, with the most obvious example being the sun.

Consider the roof of a house on a hot summer day. As the intense rays of the sun beat down on the roof hour after hour, the roof absorbs some of these radiations and converts them into heat. The amount of energy absorbed depends on the composition of the roof and the roof's color. Dark colors, such as black, will absorb more energy; light colors will reflect the sun's energy.

The heated roof transfers heat to the attic below. If the attic floor is not well-insulated, the heat in the attic is conducted rapidly into the living area below. As a result, the entire home will be heated, and air-conditioning will be required to keep it comfortable.

In winter this solar heat gain is appreciated; heating appliances do not have to work as hard to keep the house warm. Window areas allow considerable absorption of heat radiated by the sun. Unfortunately, your window areas that absorb energy so easily from the sun may also readily absorb heat radiated from objects inside the house and transfer that energy to the outside air. Stand close to a window on a cold evening. The window will absorb the heat that is radiated from your body so quickly that you will soon feel chilled. The same phenomenon occurs when the walls of a room are uninsulated and cold. A person standing or sitting near such a wall will radiate body heat to the wall and will feel cold even though the air in the room is heated to a comfortable temperature. The energy absorbed by the uninsulated walls, windows, and other exterior partitions will be conducted through the component materials and radiated to the outside environment.

MEASURING HEAT LOSS

Once you have identified how heat flows through the roof, walls, foundations, and other exterior surfaces of your house, you can calculate the amount of wasted energy (and money). Conductive and convective heat loss can be estimated rather accurately by making some simple observations and completing a few simple calculations. (**Note:** Because radiated heat loss is very difficult to measure and accounts for an insignificant percentage of the total heat loss, we will ignore radiated heat loss in our calculations.) A few simple definitions and equations are all that are really needed to make a sound estimate of the heat loss in houses and other small structures.

British Thermal Units. Heat flow is measured in *Btu* (British thermal units) per hour per square foot. A Btu is defined as the amount of heat necessary to raise 1 pound of water 1°F. A common example of the heat represented by 1 Btu is the amount of heat given off when a wooden kitchen match burns completely. One gallon of water weighs 8.34 pounds; therefore, 8.34 Btu (or 8-1/3 wooden kitchen matches) is needed to raise the temperature of 1 gallon of water 1°F.

R-Values. The rate at which conductive heat loss moves through the structural components of your home is determined by the *thermal resistance* of the various components. Thermal resistance is the measure of the ability of a material to retard heat flow, and is expressed as an *R-value*. The R-value of a material is the number of hours required for 1 Btu to be transmitted through 1 square foot of the material when there is a difference of 1°F between the ambient temperatures at each of the two surfaces of the material (Fig. 2-6). For example, polystyrene boards are available with an R-value of 5. This means that it will take 5 hours for 1 Btu of heat to pass through 1 square foot of polystyrene board when there is a 1°F difference between the air temperatures at the two opposite surfaces. Materials that have the same R-value are equal in insulating value, regardless of thickness, weight, or appearance. The higher the R-value is, the higher the insulating value. An R-value can also be an expression of the

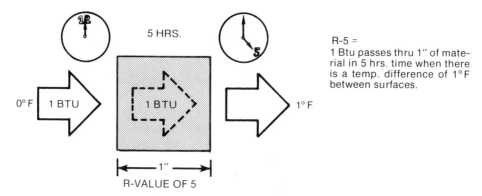

R-5 =
1 Btu passes thru 1" of material in 5 hrs. time when there is a temp. difference of 1°F between surfaces.

5 HRS.

0°F 1 BTU   1 BTU   1°F

1"

R-VALUE OF 5

Fig. 2-6: A material's ability to resist the flow of heat is indicated in R-values. The higher the R-value, the better the resistance to heat flow. An R-value is the number of hours required for the passage of 1 Btu through one square foot of 1" thick material when there is a temperature difference of 1°F between the ambient temperatures at the inside and outside surfaces.

thermal resistance of a composite of materials, such as a wall (which typically is composed of several materials). By adding together the separate R-values of each component in a wall, you know the total R-value for the wall. The R-values of many common building materials are given in Table 2-1.

U-Values. When the total R-values for the various parts of your house are known, you can determine how much heat your house is losing by conduction each hour. The overall coefficient of heat transmission is referred to as a *U-value.* U-value is the amount of heat in Btu that is transmitted through 1 square foot of a material or composite of materials, regardless of its thickness, over a period of 1 hour when there is a temperature difference of 1°F between the air on one side and the air on the other side (Fig. 2-7). It can be expressed in terms of Btu/sq ft/hr/°F. For example, a wall with a U-value of 0.3 will permit 0.3 Btu to pass through each square foot of its area over 1 hour for every 1°F difference between the inside air temperature and the outside air temperature. The lower the U-value, the higher the insulating value. The U-values of many common building materials are also given in Table 2-1.

To find the U-value of any section of your home, divide 1 by the total R-value:

$$U = 1 \div \text{total R (total of all components)}$$

For example, the U-value for a wall section with an R-value of 13.45 is calculated in this way:

$$U = 1 \div R$$
$$U = 1 \div 13.45$$
$$U = 0.074$$

A U-value of 0.074 means that for every degree of temperature difference, 0.074 Btu pass through each square foot of the wall each hour.

Annual Degree-Days. One more unit of measurement is necessary before your total heat loss can be calculated for an entire winter heating season. Total heat loss is calculated by multiplying the rate of heat loss by the annual *degree-days.* A degree-day is a unit indicating the temperature difference between the average daily temperature and an accepted standard of 65°F. Above 65°F, the heat radiated from people, appliances, and the sun will be sufficient to keep your

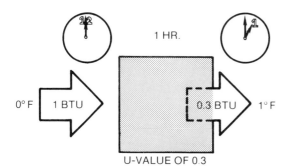

U-0.3 means that 0.3 Btu passes through the material in 1 hr. when there is a temp. difference of 1°F between the ambient temperatures at each surface.

Fig. 2-7: A U-value indicates the amount of heat in Btu that will pass through a material or composite of materials of any thickness in 1 hour when there is a temperature difference of 1°F between the air temperatures at inside and outside surfaces.

Table 2-1: R-Values and U-Values of Common Building Materials

Exterior Materials	R	U
Aluminum siding, hollow-backed	0.61	1.64
Building paper	0.06	16.7
Felt, 15#, 2 layers, mopped	0.12	8.34
Gypsum board, 1/2"	0.45	2.23
Gypsum board, 5/8"	0.56	1.78
Plywood, 1/2"	0.62	1.61
Plywood, 5/8"	0.77	1.29
Wood bevel siding, 1/2" × 8"	0.81	1.23
Wood shingles, 16", 7-1/2" exposure	0.87	1.15
Wood—maple or oak—per inch	0.91	1.09
Wood—fir or pine—per inch	1.25	0.80
Wood stud (3-1/2" fir)	4.35	0.22

Masonry Materials	R	U
Concrete blocks, three oval cores		
cinder aggregate, 8" thick	1.72	0.58
sand and gravel, 8" thick	1.11	0.90
Concrete blocks, two rectangular		
cores: sand and gravel, 8" thick	1.04	0.96
Common brick, per inch	0.20	5.0
Face brick, per inch	0.11	9.0
Sand and gravel concrete, per inch	0.08	12.5
Stucco, per inch	0.20	5.0

Roofing	R	U
Asphalt shingles	0.44	2.27
Wood shingles	0.94	1.06
Slate, 1/2"	0.05	20.0

Finish Flooring	R	U
Carpet and fibrous pad	2.08	0.48
Carpet and rubber pad	1.23	0.81
Tile: linoleum, vinyl, or rubber	0.05	20.0
Wood, hardwood finish, 3/4"	0.68	1.47

Insulation	R	U
Fiberglass, 3-1/2" thick	11.00	0.09
Fiberglass, 6" thick	19.00	0.05
Loose-fill cellulose, 3-1/2"	13.00	0.07
Polystyrene, extruded, per inch	5.40	0.19
Polyurethane, per inch	6.25	0.16

Windows and Sliding Glass Doors	R	U
Single-pane glass	0.90	1.11
Insulating glass, double-pane		
1/4" air space	1.72	0.58
1/2" air space	2.04	0.49

Table 2-1: R-Values and U-Values of Common Building Materials (Continued)

	R	U
Insulating glass, triple-pane		
1/4" air space	2.56	0.39
1/2" air space	3.23	0.31
Storm windows, 1" to 4" air space	2.00	0.50
Skylights	**R**	**U**
Single flat glass	0.81	1.23
Double-paned flat glass		
1/4" air space	1.53	0.65
1/2" air space	1.69	0.59
Plastic domes		
single-walled	0.87	1.15
double-walled	1.41	0.71
Slab Doors	**R**	**U**
Solid wood		
1" thick	1.61	0.62
1-1/4" thick	1.81	0.53
1-1/2" thick	2.13	0.47
2" thick	2.22	0.42
Solid wood with wood storm, (approximately 50% glass)		
1" thick	3.34	0.30
1-1/4" thick	3.57	0.28
1-1/2" thick	3.70	0.27
2" thick	4.17	0.24
Solid wood with metal storm		
1" thick	2.63	0.38
1-1/4" thick	2.94	0.34
1-1/2" thick	3.03	0.33
2" thick	3.44	0.29
Surface Air Films	**R**	**U**
Inside, still air		
Heat flow *up* (horizontal surface)		
nonreflective	0.61	1.64
reflective	1.32	0.75
Heat flow *down* (horizontal surface)		
nonreflective	0.92	1.08
reflective	4.55	0.22
Heat flow *horizontal* (vertical surface)		
nonreflective	0.68	1.47
reflective	1.70	0.58
Outside		
Heat flow any direction, surface any position		
15 mph wind (winter)	0.17	5.88
7.5 mph wind (summer)	0.25	4.0

house warm. The point at which there is sufficient heat may actually be even lower than 65°F in houses that are very well sealed and insulated. But a degree-day is calculated by averaging the high and low temperatures in one day and subtracting this average from 65°F. For example, on a day that has a high of 60° and a low of 40°, the average temperature is 50°. By subtracting 50° from 65°, we get 15 degree-days. The average temperature difference, then, between the outside and the inside of the house, during a single 24-hour period, is 15°F.

The sum of all the degree-days during a heating season is the total annual degree-days. The number of degree-days for a house in a given location is an indication of the relative harshness of its heating season. In the contiguous 48 states, local annual degree-day totals range from 64 (in Key West, Florida) to 13,878 (in Mt. Washington, New Hampshire). You can learn the annual degree-days in your region by calling the nearest National Weather Station.

Degree-Difference-Hours.   Degree-days cannot be used to calculate heat loss through certain structural components, such as the below-grade walls of a basement. The outside surfaces of these areas are not exposed to outside temperatures and generally have higher temperatures in winter than those exposed to the air. *Degree-difference-hours* must be used to calculate your heat loss in these areas, rather than degree-days. The degree-difference-hours (DDH) are found by multiplying the temperature difference (ΔT) between the inside temperature and the average outside temperature by the hours in a day (H) and the length of the heating season in days (L).

$$DDH = \Delta T \times H \times L$$

A call to the nearest National Weather Station will give you the number of heating days for your area. The rest is simple arithmetic.

Measuring Conductive Heat Loss

The amount of heat conducted through a material or composite of materials, such as a wall, can be calculated with four pieces of information:

1. Either the heat transmittance (U-value) or resistance to heat flow (R-value) of the wall.

2. The area (A) of the wall.

3. The difference in temperature (ΔT) between the bodies of air at each side of the wall.

4. The length of time (t) over which the heat loss occurs.

By multiplying these four factors together, the total amount of heat loss due to conduction (Q_c) can be calculated. Use one of the following equations:

$$\text{For U-values:} \quad Q_c = U \times A \times \Delta T \times t$$

$$\text{For R-values:} \quad Q_c = \frac{A \times \Delta T \times t}{R}$$

Using this formula, you can determine how much heat is conducted out of a window on a typical winter day. Suppose that the area of the window is 15 square feet, and that it consists of insulating glass with a U-value of 0.56 Btu/sq ft/hr/°F. Assuming that it is 70°F inside and 25°F outside (a temperature difference of 45°F), how much heat is lost in 1 hour?

$$Q_c = U \times A \times \Delta T \times t$$
$$Q_c = 0.56 \times 15 \times 45 \times 1$$
$$Q_c = 378 \text{ Btu per hour}$$

Compare the loss from the 15 square foot window to that of the 80 square foot wall around it. The wall is insulated to an R-value of 13.74. If the temperature difference (ΔT) is still 45°F, the heat lost through the wall in 1 hour is:

$$Q_c = \frac{A \times \Delta T \times t}{R}$$

$$Q_c = \frac{80 \times 45 \times 1}{13.74}$$

$$Q_c = 262 \text{ Btu per hour}$$

As you can see, even small windows represent comparatively large heat losses.

To calculate the conductive heat loss for the entire house, each part—each wall, door, window, floor or foundation, and ceiling—is evaluated separately. The results are then added together for the total. The area of each component is measured and the total R-value through a section of its materials is determined. Table 2-2 lists the heat loss for various parts of a 1,400 square foot ranch-style house. Total R-values are converted to U-values in this example.

Table 2-2: Total Conductive Heat Loss

	U–Value ×	Square Feet ×	ΔT =	Btu/hr Loss
Exterior walls (3)	0.07	1,230	45	3,875
Wall shared with garage	0.07	220	35	539
Windows (double-glazed)	0.56	160	45	4,032
Doors (2 exterior w/storms)	0.33	30	45	446
Ceiling	0.05	1,400	30	2,100
Floor	0.07	1,400	20	1,960
		Conductive Heat Loss for the House =		12,952 Btu/hr

Note in Fig. 2-8 that the temperature difference (ΔT) will usually be different for each part of the house. The exterior walls, for example, are subjected to colder temperatures than a wall shared with a garage, or a floor over the basement.

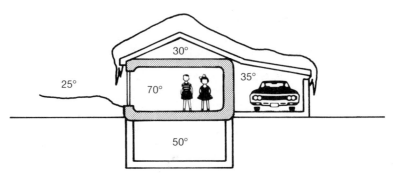

Fig. 2-8: Unheated areas that are not exposed to outside air are generally slightly warmer than outside temperatures. Degree-difference-hours must be used to calculate heat loss into these areas.

Measuring Convective Heat Loss

Even in a well-insulated, tightly sealed house, the heat lost by convection may be 30% or more of the total heat loss. In older homes or in homes in which infiltration has not been reduced by caulking and weatherstripping, the percentage of heat loss due to infiltration is much higher. Exactly how much heat you are losing through cracks and openings is difficult to determine.

Since the size and number of cracks cannot be determined, the air pressure inside and outside the house is in constant fluctuation, and average wind speed is variously affected by local geography and obstructions. Professional auditors and heating contractors make *estimates* based on educated guesswork. There are two methods for estimating infiltration heat loss: the *air change method* and the *crack method.* The results of both methods are approximate. The crack method estimates heat loss by adding up the total length of window and door perimeters and predicting the infiltration rate based on published air leakage values for the windows and doors under evaluation. The air change method assumes a certain number of *air changes per hour* (ACH) within the house, and calculates the resulting heat loss.

An *air change* is the complete replacement of conditioned air with outside air by exfiltration and infiltration. Even a well-sealed home on a calm day may have 20% of its air replaced every hour. On windy days the air change rate will go higher. The estimate of air changes per hour can range from as low as 0.35 to as high as 5; however, some studies have documented air changes outside this range. A number of factors affect the ACH for a given house (Table 2-3). These include the size and length of cracks at windows and doors; the number and size of chimneys, vents, exhaust fans, etc., and the frequency of their use; the frequency and period of time in which doors and windows are opened; the average speed of the wind, wind protection. The following values can be used for general calculations:

> 2 to 3 ACH—drafty, uninsulated house
> 1.5 ACH—most older houses
> 1.0 ACH—standard new house
> 0.5 ACH—tightly constructed new house

Table 2-3: Typical Features of Buildings Having Various Air Changes per Hour

Building Component	One Air Change per Hour	Two Air Changes per Hour	Three Air Changes per Hour
Building with cellar or	Tight, no cracks, caulked sills, sealed cellar windows, no grade entrance leaks.	Some foundation cracks, no weather-stripping on cellar windows, grade entrance not tight.	Stone foundation, considerable leakage area, poor seal around grade entrance.
Building with crawl space or on posts	Plywood floor, no trap door leaks, no leaks around water, sewer, and electrical openings.	Tongue-and-groove board floor, reasonable fit on trap doors, around pipes, etc.	Board floor, loose fit around pipes, etc.
Windows	Storm windows with good fit.	No storm windows, good fit on regular windows.	No storm windows, loose fit on regular windows.
Doors	Good fit on storm doors.	Loose storm doors, poor fit on side door.	No storm doors, loose fit on inside door.
Walls	Caulked windows and doors, building paper used under siding.	Caulking in poor repair.	No indication of building paper, evident cracks around doorframe and window frame.

To build a home with an infiltration rate below 1.0 ACH requires special care in design and construction. Rates below 0.5 ACH are *very* difficult to achieve.

To calculate infiltration using the air change method, the following five factors must be considered:

1. Volume (V) of air in the house.
2. Number of air changes per hour (ACH).
3. Heating capacity of air (HC). **Note:** The heating capacity of air is equal to the amount of heat in Btu necessary to raise the temperature of one cubic foot of air 1°F. For our calculations, we will use the value 0.020.
4. Temperature difference between inside and outside air (ΔT).
5. Length of time (t) over which heat loss occurs.

The product of these five factors equals the quantity of heat lost due to air infiltration (Q_i), expressed in Btu.

$$Q_i = V \times ACH \times HC \times \Delta T \times t$$

For an example of the amount of heat that can escape from a home by way of infiltration and exfiltration, calculate the convective heat loss for the sample ranch-style house mentioned on page 17. The house has 8' walls; therefore, the volume of air in the house is 11,200 cubic feet (which is arrived at by multiplying the area by the height: 1,400 ft² × 8 ft = 11,200 ft³). Since the house is relatively new, it has an estimated air change rate of 1.0. How much heat is lost by infiltration per hour if the interior is 70°, and the outside temperature is 25°?

$$Q_i = V \times ACH \times HC \times \Delta T \times t$$
$$Q_i = 11,200 \times 1.0 \times 0.020 \times 45 \times 1$$
$$Q_i = 10,080 \text{ Btu}$$

Calculating Total Heat Loss

Total heat loss can be found by substituting annual degree-days (DD) or degree-difference-hours (DDH) for temperature difference (ΔT) in our equations. The loss is calculated using 24-hour periods rather than the 1-hour time spans we used in our earlier calculations. The equations for figuring total conductive heat loss (Q_c) and total heat loss due to infiltration (Q_i) are given here:

$$Q_c \quad = U \times A \times DD \times 24 \text{ hrs/day}$$
$$Q_c \quad = U \times A \times DDH$$
$$Q_i \quad = V \times ACH \times HC \times DD \times 24 \text{ hrs/day}$$
$$Q_{total} = Q_c + Q_i = \text{Heat Loss per Year (Btu)}$$

To illustrate, let us assume as our example, a 1,400 square foot ranch-style house, located in Boston, Massachusetts, that has a heating season of 5,600 annual degree-days. The conductive heat loss for the exterior walls is figured this way:

$$Q_c = U \times A \times DD \times 24 \text{ hrs/day}$$
$$Q_c = 0.07 \times 1,230 \times 5,600 \times 24$$
$$Q_c = 11,571,840 \text{ Btu}$$

Since annual degree-days can only be used to calculate total heat loss through surface areas exposed to outside air temperatures, degree-difference-hours must be used to calculate total heat loss through the surface areas that separate heated living spaces and from unheated areas such as the garage and basement.

To calculate heat loss through floors over an unheated basement, you must first determine the temperature of the basement. This is best done during the heating season. In our sample house, the basement remains at about 50°F all winter. The temperature difference when the house is heated to 70°F is 20°F. Multiplied by the length of the heating season (for example, 250 days), and by the hours in a day, the degree-difference-hours (DDH) are calculated as:

$$20°F \times 250 \times 24 = 120,000$$

The 120,000 degree-difference-hours is then multiplied by the U-value of the floor, and the total floor area, to determine the annual heat loss through the floor. The floor area in our sample house is 1,400 square feet. The U-value is found by first considering the characteristics of each of the various materials in the floor. If there were more than one kind of floor, the area and heat loss of each type must be figured separately. Our sample house has wall-to-wall carpeting over a foam pad in every room. Figure 2-9 shows a sectional view of the floor and gives the total R-value.

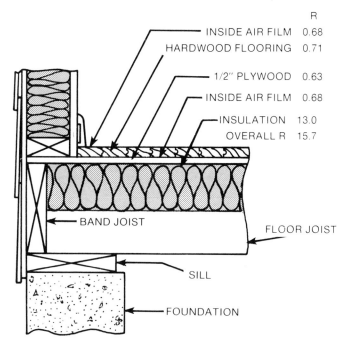

	R
INSIDE AIR FILM	0.68
HARDWOOD FLOORING	0.71
1/2" PLYWOOD	0.63
INSIDE AIR FILM	0.68
INSULATION	13.0
OVERALL R	15.7

BAND JOIST

FLOOR JOIST

SILL

FOUNDATION

Fig. 2-9: The R-values of the components in the floor combine to give a total R-value of 15.7.

With an R-value of 15.7, the U-value of the floor is 0.064 (U = 1 ÷ R). To find the total heat loss, multiply U-values by the square footage and again by degree-difference-hours. The result will be:

$$0.064 \times 1,400 \times 120,000 = 10,752,000 \text{ Btu}$$

Using either annual degree-days or degree-difference-hours, calculate the conductive heat loss through each surface area that separates a heated living space from an unheated area. The sum total of these areas plus the convective heat loss is the total heat loss for your house. Do not be surprised if the number of Btu is over a hundred million. The *average* New England home consumes 176 million Btu each year.

ESTIMATING ENERGY EFFICIENCY

With these energy basics in mind, you are equipped to analyze the energy needs of your home and make the most efficient use of weatherproofing and energy-saving techniques. Once the energy leaks are located, the preceding information will make it possible to determine how much money the leaks are costing, and how much energy a particular technique will save. For example, the typical uninsulated frame home has an R-value of 3.34 and a U-value of 0.29 (Fig. 2-10A). By adding 3-1/2" of blown-in cellulose, the R-value increases to 15.5 and the U-value decreases to 0.064 (Fig. 2-10B). With the equations given

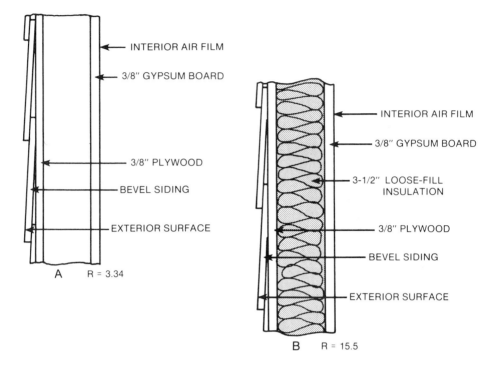

Fig. 2-10: (A) The typical uninsulated 2 by 4 frame wall has an R-value of 3.34. (B) Adding 3-1/2" of blown-in cellulose raises the R-value to 15.5.

already in this chapter, you can figure the difference in total heat loss and, thus, determine how much energy and money you can save by insulating the walls. In a region with 6,000 annual degree-days, the uninsulated wall will lose 41,760 Btu per square foot each heating season. But the insulated wall would lose only 9,216 Btu per square foot during the season. At 6¢/Kwh, insulating the wall will save 57¢/sq. ft. during each heating season.

Making a Home Energy Audit 3

The objectives of home weatherproofing are quite simple. It is used to: (1) slow down the rate of conductive heat flow through the shell of your house and (2) eliminate the cracks through which infiltration and exfiltration occur. The techniques and materials used to accomplish these objectives are uncomplicated and, as you will see in later chapters, the proper use of many types of adhesives and glues simplifies the task of weatherproofing even more. The purpose of this chapter, *Making a Home Energy Audit*, is to help you find out *where* your home is in need of weatherproofing.

A home energy audit is simply a detailed inspection of your house in search of insufficient insulation and sources of infiltrating air. It requires only simple tools—a flashlight, a ruler, a coat hanger, etc. The largest investment you will make will be in time. Take as much time as is necessary to inspect every area of your house. Get to know your home inside and out. Learn how it functions day and night, in every season of the year, and in all kinds of weather. A good home energy audit will ''see'' the house from several perspectives. It will require searching on hands and knees for cracks around baseboards and electrical outlets, poking into corners and crawl spaces in search of insulation. It will also demand standing back and studying the relationship of the house to nearby hills, buildings, and bodies of water. How do these objects in the surrounding landscape affect the home's exposure to prevailing winds and direct sunlight? The answers to these questions are important factors in understanding the energy efficiency of your home and in determining which weatherproofing techniques to apply.

SEARCHING FOR INSULATION

Figure 3-1 pinpoints the areas of your house that should be insulated. Insulation should always separate warm-in-winter living areas from unheated areas and from the outside. For example, if your basement is unheated, insulation should be placed in the floor between the cold basement and the heated living area above. If the basement is heated, insulation should be placed on the basement wall, separating the warm basement from the cold exterior.

The amount of insulation needed in ceilings, walls, and floors varies according to the climate in which you live. Table 3-1, developed by the U.S. Department of Energy, recommends *minimum* insulation standards for home retrofit. The R-values given should be considered target levels that can be met or exceeded by any kind of insulation.

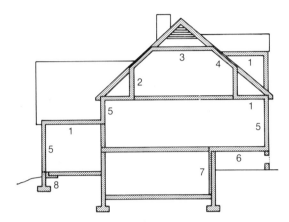

Fig. 3-1: Areas that should be insulated are: (1) ceilings below any unheated attic spaces; (2) knee walls; (3) collar beams; (4) attic rafters; (5) exterior walls; (6) floors over unheated crawl spaces; (7) walls of a heated basement; and (8) foundation perimeters of on-grade slab floor.

To use Table 3-1, find the zone in which you live on the map shown in Fig. 3-2. Then, use the R-values given. But, keep in mind that these are minimum R-value recommendations. If the climate is extremely cold, or if air conditioning is used extensively, the cost of energy will be higher, so that these resistance values should be *significantly* increased (as shown in Table 3-2). Zone A should follow the recommendations of Zone B for optimum savings during the cooling season.

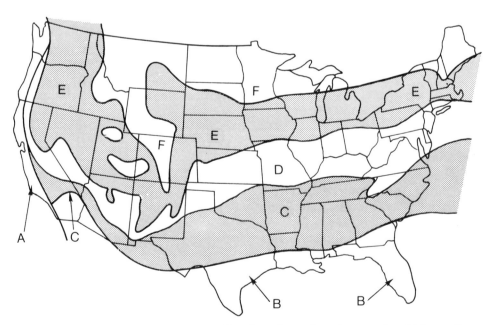

Fig. 3-2: Minimum and recommended R-values depend on the zone in which you live.

Table 3-1: Minimum Recommended R-Values

Heating Degree-Days	Attic Floors		Ceilings over Unheated Crawl Space or Basement			Crawl Space Walls		
	Oil, Gas, Electric Heat Pump	Electric Resistance Heat	Oil, Gas	Electric Heat Pump	Electric Resistance Heat	Oil, Gas, Electric Heat Pump	Electric Resistance Heat	Exterior Walls*
1001-2500 (Zone B)	30	30	11	11	19	11	19	11
2501-3500 (Zone C)	30	30	11	11	19	11	19	11
3501-6000 (Zone D)	30	30	11	19	19	19	19	11
6001-7000 (Zone E)	30	38	11	19	19	19	19	11
7001 and above (Zone F)	38	38	19	19	19	19	19	11

*R-value of full wall insulation, which is 3-1/2" thick, will depend on material used. Range is R–11 to R–13.

Table 3-2: Recommended R-Values

Winter Heating

Zone	Attic Floor (Ceilings)	Side Walls	Floors
B	R-30 (10")	R-13 (3-1/2" Full Wall)	R-11 (3-1/2")
C	R-30 (10")	R-13 (3-1/2" Full Wall)	R-11 (3-1/2")
D	R-30-38 (10" or 12")	R-19 (6")	R-19 (6")
E	R-38 (12")	R-19 (6")	R-19 (6")
F	R-49 (15-1/2")	R-19 (6")	R-19 (6")

Summer Cooling Plus Winter Heating

Zone	Attic Floor (Ceilings)	Side Walls	Floors
B	R-30 (10")	R-13 (3-1/2" Full Wall)	R-13 (3-1/2" Full Wall)
C	R-30 (10")	R-13 (3-1/2" Full Wall)	R-13 (3-1/2" Full Wall)
D	R-38 (12")	R-19 (6")	R-19 (6")
E	R-38 (12")	R-19 (6")	R-19 (6")
F	R-49 (15-1/2")	R-19 (6")	R-19 (6")

Determining the amount of insulation already present in your home is easy in some areas and difficult in others. Insulation is exposed to view in unfinished attic floors and basement ceilings, but is hidden in finished walls and ceilings. Discovering how much insulation these inaccessible areas contain will require a little more work.

Measuring Attic Insulation

In an unfinished attic, the amount of insulation between the ceiling joists is not difficult to determine. If the insulation you find there is faced batts or blankets, the R-value will be printed on the vapor barrier facing. Simply lift the batt and find the information printed underneath. If the insulation is unfaced batts or blankets or if it is a type of loose-fill, the insulation must be measured and the R-value calculated. Slip a ruler down alongside the ceiling joist and record the depth of the insulation (Fig. 3-3A). Determine the total R-value of the insulation, multiplying the depth by the R-value per inch of the material (see Table 9-1 in Chapter 9, *Choosing and Buying Insulation*). For example, you inspect your unheated attic and find that there are 4" of loose-fill rock wool (R-3.0) between the joists. The R-value of the installed insulation is:

$$4'' \times 3.0 = 12$$
$$R = 12$$

Table 3-3 lists approximate R-values for varying depths of attic insulation.

If your attic has a finished floor, the insulation will be hidden from view. Try prying up a board in an inconspicuous spot, or bore a hole through the flooring. The insulation can then be measured.

If the attic has been finished into a living space, crawl behind the walls and measure the insulation between the studs and the ceiling rafters. If a hatch leads into the area above the collar beams, climb into this area and measure the insulation between the collar beams as you would measure insulation in an attic floor.

Table 3-3: R-Values According to Depth of Attic Insulation

	Batts or Blankets		Loose-Fill (Poured In)		
	glass fiber	rock wool	glass fiber	rock wool	cellulosic fiber
R-11	3-1/2"—4"	3"	5"	4"	3"
R-13	4"	4-1/2"	6"	4-1/2"	3-1/2"
R-19	6"—6-1/2"	5-1/4"	8"—9"	6"—7"	5"
R-22	6-1/2"	6"	10"	7"—8"	6"
R-26	8"	8-1/2"	12"	9"	7"—7-1/2"
R-30	9-1/2"—10-1/2"	9"	13"—14"	10"—11"	8"
R-33	11"	10"	15"	11"—12"	9"
R-38	12"—13"	10-1/2"	17"—18"	13"—14"	10"—11"

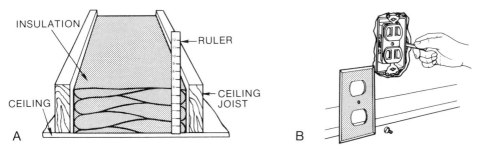

Fig. 3-3: Measuring insulation thickness. (A) A ruler can be used to measure the depth of insulation between the ceiling joists. (B) To measure wall insulation thickness use a clothes hanger wire or a pencil. **CAUTION:** *Be sure the supply of electricity to the outlet is turned off.*

Roofs without attics, such as flat or sloped roofs, are usually standard roof joists covered below with drywall and above with plywood roof decking and roof material, making the roof construction similar to that of walls, with cavities between the joists. If there is no access into the roof cavity, make a small opening about 6" by 6" in a closet ceiling, and measure the insulation. **CAUTION:** Be careful not to cut electrical wires.

Measuring Wall Insulation

Walls are sometimes difficult to inspect for insulation. Sometimes in a balloon frame house, the tops of the walls will be open in the attic. If this is the case in your house, use a flashlight and peer down into the cavity to locate any insulation that might be visible. Another way to discover insulation in walls is to remove an electrical outlet or switch cover and to probe into the wall cavity with the curved end of a clothes hanger or a pencil (Fig. 3-3B). **CAUTION:** Turn off the electricity at the fuse box, first! Do the same thing around vents and registers in your walls. You can also cut a hole into the wall behind a baseboard. The baseboard will hide the hole when the trim is replaced. If your probing collects any fibrous material, the wall has at least some insulation. In the search for insulation, do not overlook the walls that separate heated rooms from unheated rooms, such as garages or utility rooms.

Measuring Basement Insulation

The basement may have insulation in several places. If the basement is unheated, measure the amount of insulation in the ceiling (Fig. 3-4). If the insulation is properly installed, the vapor barrier will be against the subfloor above. Pull the insulation back and locate the R-value printed on the vapor barrier. Or measure with a ruler and calculate the total R-value as you did for the attic floor. Also, look for insulated pipes and ducts. All hot water pipes and hot air ducts in unheated spaces should be insulated. Determine whether or not the hot water heater has an insulated jacket. If not, the water heater should also be insulated.

Fig. 3-4: The R-value of basement ceiling insulation is printed on the vapor barrier facing.

Crawl spaces should be insulated. Unheated spaces should have insulation in the floor joists above. If the crawl space (or basement) is heated, the insulation should be on the walls of the space (Fig. 3-5).

An area that may be overlooked in a heated basement or crawl space is the band joist. The band joist is an upright 2 by 8 or 2 by 10 that sits atop the sole plate. Check to see if the wall insulation extends up to cover the band joist.

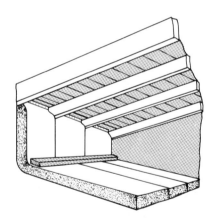

Fig. 3-5: The walls and band joist of a heated crawl space should be insulated.

SEARCHING FOR INFILTRATION

Do not fall into the trap of thinking that insulation is a cure-all for energy waste problems. Most of the heat loss in an average non-energy-efficient home is a result of infiltration and exfiltration. If the cracks and crevices are not caulked and weatherstripped before adding insulation, air will simply bypass the insulation; therefore, discovering the sources of air infiltration into the living areas of your home is very important.

The search for infiltration requires a few simple tools. An important one is a flashlight. Often you can see light penetrating through a crack even when you cannot discern air movement. Another tool for detecting slight air movements is an incense stick. The smoke given off by the smoldering stick will follow the slightest air movement. If you would rather not use a burning incense stick around combustible materials, you can make a simple (and safe) infiltration detector with a clothes hanger, a piece of tissue, and two clothes pins (Fig. 3-6). Hold the detector in front of any suspected crack and any movement in the tissue will indicate air infiltration.

If possible, conduct your search for infiltration on a windy day. The stronger the wind, the easier it will be to detect infiltrating air.

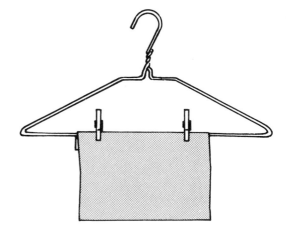

Fig. 3-6: A simple infiltration detector can be made from a coat hanger, two clothes pins, and a sheet of tissue.

Penetrations into the Interior

Begin searching for areas of infiltration inside your house. Listed here are some of the places where you are most likely to discover air seeping into your home.

● Basement—sole plate, windows, doors, clothes dryer vents, pipe and wire penetrations.

● Living spaces—windows, doors, electrical outlets, wall switches, baseboards, ceiling moldings, corner moldings, wainscoating, recessed lights, pipe and vent penetrations, flues and fireplace dampers.

● Attic—recessed light fixtures, vents, flues, chimneys.

Penetrations through the Exterior

One of the most important places to search for sources of infiltration is the exterior of your home (Fig. 3-7). A leisurely stroll around the house will turn up a variety of penetrations and seams. Every place an outside faucet pipe, electrical wire, telephone wire, or antenna cable enters the house is a place that needs sealing. The seams where construction materials meet should be sealed. These include the junction of siding and window frames and doorframes, the junction of brick veneer and siding, the junction of chimney and siding, the junction of the sole plate and the foundation, and the junction of two walls. Every seam in the house permits air to enter the walls and seep into living spaces. Look for cracks in

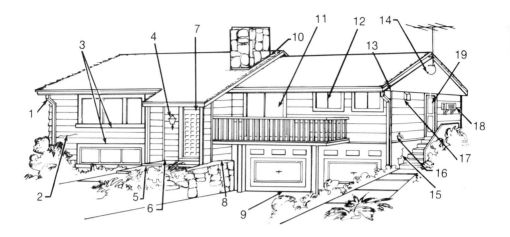

Fig. 3-7: Areas that should be sealed are: (1) downspouts; (2) cracks in siding; (3) window frames; (4) exterior lights; (5) sole plates; (6) junctions on siding; (7) entrance doors; (8) junctions of dissimilar construction materials; (9) garage door bottoms; (10) chimneys; (11) sliding doors; (12) window sashes; (13) soffits; (14) wire penetrations; (15) cracks in foundations; (16) pipe penetrations; (17) exhaust vents; (18) air conditioner penetrations; and (19) storm doors.

the foundation walls and for small holes where mortar between the bricks or blocks has fallen out.

WHAT TO DO FIRST

After completing the tour of your home in search of insufficient insulation and infiltrating air, make a list of the problem areas you found. Decide what steps should be taken to correct the problems. Then, determine the order in which to tackle each problem. Setting priorities is often a troublesome task, especially when only a limited amount of money is available to invest in weatherproofing. Setting priorities is easier if you make decisions on the basis of the following factors involved in saving energy and money.

● *Cost.* How much money will a particular project cost? Do only what you can afford.

● *Lifetime.* How long will the particular weatherstripping technique last?

● *Yearly Savings.* How much energy and money will you save the first year?

● *Lifetime Benefit.* How much of a savings will you realize over the lifetime of the particular product?

● *Payback.* How many years will it take for the savings in energy costs to equal the initial cost of the weatherproofing technique? A payback period of more than seven years is not considered a wise investment.

Discuss these concerns with your insulation dealer or heating and cooling specialist, who can help you make the best choice of weatherproofing techniques. With these factors known for each weatherproofing project, you can wisely set priorities.

Adhesives and Weatherizing 4

As mentioned in Chapter 1, adhesives and glues play a major role in many weatherizing projects, particularly those involving the expansion or remodeling of your home's living areas. Many general adhesives are formulated to provide good bonding on a wide range of materials, and more specialized glues and adhesives meet the exact needs of highly specific bonding jobs. For example, there are specially formulated construction adhesives designed to bond drywall to wood framing members; plywood sheathing to floor joists; rigid foam board insulation to concrete, furring strips, or wood-based materials; paneling to rigid foam board insulation; paneling to metal studs or furring strips; and acoustic ceiling tiles to furring strips. For more detailed information, see the author's book *Home Construction Projects with Adhesives and Glues*.

This specialization has taken some of the mystery out of selecting an adhesive or glue for use in a home weatherizing or remodeling project. The information found in this chapter will give you the background knowledge needed to match one of today's specialized adhesives and glues to the job you have in mind. When using any adhesive or glue, follow the general instructions and safety precautions given in this book and all manufacturer's instructions and precautions printed on the adhesive can, container, or cartridge.

SELECTION OF THE RIGHT ADHESIVE

Selecting the correct adhesive or glue for the job involves considering several important points. For instance, the temperature to which the adhesive will be subjected can severely affect its performance. A few adhesives can be used at both high and low temperatures, while others only perform well within certain temperature ranges. Most adhesives will not bond if the surface to which they are applied is not properly cleaned and prepared; other adhesives need no special preparation. Many adhesives have a strong initial grab and fast drying time; others dry slowly and require that the bonded surface be held tightly together until the adhesive cures.

Consider the Materials Joined

What types of materials will be fastened? Are the materials to be joined porous or nonporous? Wood, cork, gypsum, and concrete blocks are considered porous materials, while metal, glass, ceramics, porcelain, tile, some poured concretes, and most plastic foams are nonporous. Are you trying to join two dissimilar materials such as wood and plastic foam? Are the materials rigid or flexible? Are the materials being bonded smooth or rough? Are they compatible with each other and with the adhesive?

A vivid example of the importance of matching the proper adhesive with the materials being bonded is shown in Fig. 4-1. The solvent or base of many construction adhesives may attack polystyrene plastic foam and "eat" a hole right through it. Only an adhesive that is designed and marketed for bonding polystyrene should be used with the material. Table 4-1 identifies the types of adhesives and glues that are used to bond various construction materials.

Table 4-1: Selecting an Adhesive

Bonding to	Masonry	Ceramics	Metal Foils	Paper Surfaces	Rubber	Felts
Wood	a, c, e	a, b, c, d, e	b, d	a, b, c, d, e, f	a, b, c, d, e, f	a, b, c, d, e, f
Glass	a, c	a, b, c, d	d	a, b, c, d, e, f	a, b, c, d, e, f	a, b, c, d, e, f
Metal	a, b, c, d	a, b, c, d	d	a, b, c, d, e, f	a, b, c, d, e, f	a, b, c, d, e, f
Plastic Laminates	a, b, c, d	a, b, c, d	d	a, b, c, d, e, f	a, b, c, d, e, f	a, b, c, d, e, f
Fabrics	b, d, f	b, d, f	b, d	b, d, f	b, d, f	b, d, f
Rigid Plastics	a, b, c, d	a, b, c, d	d	a, b, c, d, e, f	d	a, b, c, d, e, f
Plastic Films	f	f	f	f	f	f
Polystyrene Foam	e, f	e, f	f	e, f	f	e, f
Polyurethane Foam	a, b, c, d, e, f	a, b, c, d, e, f	b, d, f	a, b, c, d, e, f	a, b, c, d, e, f	a, b, c, d, e, f
Felts	b, d, f	b, d, f	b, d, f	b, d, f	b, d, f	b, d, f
Rubber	b, d, f	b, d, f	b, d, f	b, d, f	d, f	
Paper Surfaces	a, b, c, d, e, f	a, b, c, d, e, f	d, f	a, b, c, d, e, f		
Metal Foils	b, d	b, d	d, f			
Ceramics	a, c, e	a, b, c				
Masonry	a, c					

Notes: a. Synthetic rubber elastomers, solvent base, high viscosity.
 b. Synthetic rubber elastomers, solvent base, low viscosity.
 c. Neoprene elastomers, solvent base, high viscosity.
 d. Neoprene elastomers, solvent base, low viscosity.
 e. Synthetic polymers, water base, high viscosity.
 f. Neoprene latex and latex resin emulsions, water base, low viscosity.

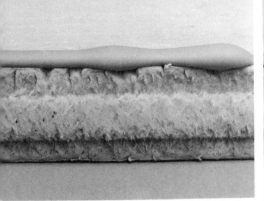

Fig. 4-1: The solvents in many adhesives will chemically attack polystyrene and certain other foams and cause the insulation to dissolve or disintegrate.

Table 4-1: Selecting an Adhesive (Continued)

Poly- urethane Foam	Poly- styrene Foam	Plastic Films	Rigid Plastics	Fabrics	Plastic Laminates	Metal	Glass	Wood
a, b, c, d, e, f	a, f	f	a, b, c, d, e, f	d, f	a, b, c, d, e, f	a, b, c, d, e, f	a, b, c, d, e, f	a, b, c, d, e, f
d, f	f	f	d, f	d, f	d, f	d, f	d, f	
d, f	f	f	d, f	d, f	d, f	d, f		
d, f	f	f	d, f	d, f	d, f			
b, d, f	f	f	d, f	d, f				
d, f	f	f	d, f					
f	f	f						
f	f							
d, f								

Consider Physical Conditions and Characteristics

Will the completed bond be subjected to heat, cold, or moisture? Are there large voids that require a gap-filling function by the adhesive? To what kind of stress will the finished joint be subjected? Is the glue flammable? Are the materials structurally sound or are there internal weaknesses that will affect the strengths? What is the color of the adhesive when it is dried? Will any surface preparations be required to provide an adequate bonding surface? Is drying time important? Where is the bonding taking place? If you are working in an area with poor ventilation, you do not want to use an adhesive with a toxic, flammable, or explosive effect.

Follow Manufacturer's Recommendations

The adhesive manufacturer's recommendations and precautions must be carefully weighed against the factors involved in the selection process, and any specific information given by the manufacturer should be followed precisely. Always remember that the recommendations given by the manufacturer will provide the most successful bonding results. However, it may still be necessary to use a good amount of personal judgment and common sense when deciding upon a particular adhesive or glue for a specific project. Although the manufacturer's suggestions for the uses of a particular adhesive are usually valid, there may be instances when a product designed for a specific application will be better for the job at hand than a multipurpose adhesive that is also recommended for the job. In addition, the claims on a container of adhesive can often be interpreted in several ways. For example, there is no real dividing line between a product that is truly waterproof, stainproof, or heat-resistant and one that is not. What amount of immersion in water will destroy a glue bond? At what temperature will an adhesive fail? It is probable that the manufacturer knows these limitations, but the average do-it-yourselfer does not. Therefore, it is a good idea to use widely known adhesive products with which you can feel confident that the manufacturer's claims will hold true.

The adhesive label on the container, besides containing the manufacturer's instructions, also carries other important information (Fig. 4-2). For instance, some solvent-based adhesives may be extremely flammable and contain dangerous toxic fumes. As a result, the Consumer Product Safety Commission has placed a ban on consumer sales of extremely flammable contact cements. You can recognize these glues on your shelf by required warnings, such as "Danger, Extremely Flammable, Keep Away From Children." If you still have some of these on your shelf, follow these precautions when using them: Do not smoke, turn off all pilot lights, and work in a well-ventilated room.

Many manufacturers now produce a water-based or nonflammable version of flammable adhesives. This is especially true of contact cements. The flammable types dry faster than the water or emulsion systems because the solvents evaporate faster. However, there are now nonflammable solvents, utilizing chlorinated solvent systems, that will dry equally as fast as their flammable counterparts. These are becoming quite common in contact cements and floor-

Fig. 4-2: Carefully follow the manufacturer's instructions and heed any warnings printed on the label.

ing adhesives. All three types are nearly equal in effectiveness as adhesives. The nonflammable types, though, eliminate both the fire hazard and certain other hazards associated with volatile solvent systems. Caution should be exercised in the use of the nonflammable chlorinated solvent systems, and prolonged inhalation should be avoided. Tools used with the water-based type can generally be cleaned with soap and water while the glue is still wet.

CONSTRUCTION ADHESIVES FOR USE IN WEATHERPROOFING

In these days of high building costs, the construction industry has found that adhesives not only save time and materials, but also do the job better. Fortunately, most of these advantages of using adhesives in residential and commercial construction can also be realized by the do-it-yourselfer.

General construction adhesives (Fig. 4-3) dry exceptionally fast (10 to 30 minutes working time) at normal temperatures (above 60°F).In cold temperatures, drying will be somewhat retarded. Do not apply at temperatures below 10°F. Many formulations can be used for both interior and exterior applications.

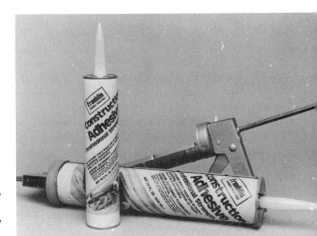

Fig. 4-3: General or multi-purpose construction adhesives can be used in many applications. They have the versatility and performance required for any building or remodeling job.

The adhesive can be gun extruded (using a caulking gun) or applied with a spatula or putty knife; some are designed for trowel applications. Their high degree of initial tack allows light pieces to be bonded with only momentary pressure. Exposure of the adhesive to air before assembly will increase this initial grab. The allowable open time is regulated by the temperature, humidity, air circulation, and the basic characteristics of the formulation. Most construction adhesives are heavy viscosity formulations that help to fill gaps and bridge minor framing irregularities. Many of the modern construction adhesives are nonflammable and nontoxic, while others contain volatile solvents such as hexane, acetone, and toluene. When applying the latter, do not use near fire or flame (spark), and use only with adequate ventilation. Since some construction adhesives attack polystyrene foams, always check the manufacturer's recommendations on the container before using them on this material.

Construction adhesives can be divided into two broad categories: those with a solvent base and those with a water base. The solvent-based adhesives have a much faster drying time and a higher initial tack. Water-based adhesives are important in the consideration of insulation, because they are compatible with polystyrene foam insulation, while many solvent-based adhesives are not. Usually the liquid portion, whether solvent or water, is clearly identified on the label. If there is some confusion as to what the base is, a water-based adhesive can often be identified by the words "latex" or "emulsion" and by the caution on the label to avoid freezing.

The following paragraphs describe some of the common construction adhesives and how they can be used in any weatherproofing, remodeling project.

Metal Framing and Structural Adhesives

These products frequently use a neoprene base. They are designed to meet the growing demands of galvanized steel and aluminum framing members in both floor and wall systems (Fig. 4-4). Many develop exceptional strength when

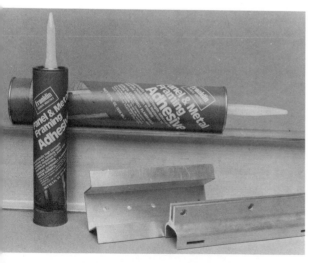

Fig. 4-4: Metal framing and structural adhesives can be used to bond a variety of construction materials to metal studs.

bonding plywood, gypsum wallboard, hardboard, and paneling to these metal surfaces. Generally speaking, neoprene adhesives have high temperature resistance and extremely long-range aging characteristics. They remain permanently resilient through wide temperature variations from –40°F to 200°F. Initial tack is quite high. The creep resistance is also unusually high on some formulations. But, remember that since a flammable solvent system is employed with these adhesives, they are flammable and their vapors can be harmful. Performance characteristics do vary widely from manufacturer to manufacturer, so be sure you read and understand the label.

Neoprene adhesives are valuable when bonding insulation to metal buildings and other metal surfaces where extremely hot temperatures are encountered. Neoprenes with a water base are available for use with polystyrene foam insulation.

Panel Adhesives

These adhesives, frequently called panel and plywood adhesives as well as by other names (Fig. 4-5), can be used to bond panels, gypsum drywall, hardboard, corkboard, bulletin boards, or chalkboards to masonry, studs, drywall, or concrete. Paneling of all types can be bonded tightly to studs, drywall, masonry, or furring strips with these adhesives and requires few or no nails for a smooth, one-step installation. This eliminates nail pops and patching, plus removes the danger of marring prefinished panels with hammer marks. Panel adhesives also overcome structural deficiencies, fill gaps, and bridge minor framing irregularities. Usually dispensed from cartridges, most panel adhesives will not drip from beams or sag from vertical surfaces. Most panel adhesives are synthetic rubber elastomers with solvent bases that may not be compatible with polystyrene foam. But, never use a panel adhesive to bond paneling to polystyrene unless the label specifically recommends such an application.

Fig. 4-5: A panel adhesive may eliminate the need for nailing.

Foam Board Adhesives

Plastic foams, both polystyrene and polyurethane, are being used more frequently today in all types of construction. Because the polystyrene reacts chemically with many solvents, adhesives have been specially formulated for bonding plastic foam insulation to construction materials (Fig. 4-6). Be absolutely certain that the adhesive you are using is designated by the manufacturer as being satisfactory for use on polystyrene foams. If not, it can ruin your entire installation, resulting in complete failure of your wall or ceiling system. Certain solvents, however, can be used and there are some solvent-based adhesive formulations on the market that are perfectly satisfactory. Those with an emulsion (water) base are generally the best choice, since water will not attack the foam.

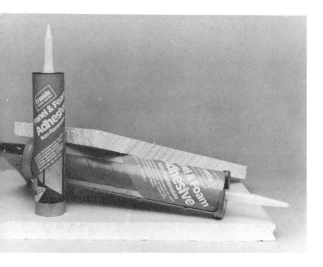

Fig. 4-6: Rigid board insulation should be applied with a panel and foam adhesive specially formulated to be compatible with plastic foam insulations.

Polyurethane (or urethane) foams, on the other hand, are not widely used for insulation in the consumer markets, particularly on do-it-yourself types of projects. They are considerably more expensive than the polystyrenes, although a lesser thickness will generally provide as much insulation value as a greater thickness of polystyrene. Currently, the largest use for urethane in the home construction area is in simulated wood beams for ceilings. Urethane foams have a great deal of resistance to most of the solvents used in adhesives; therefore, a good construction or panel adhesive will work nicely with the urethanes.

To distinguish between polystyrene and polyurethane, apply a few good "rules of thumb." Urethanes are generally of a yellowish color and have a smaller or finer pore structure. Polystyrenes, on the other hand, are generally white or blue. They may or may not have a small or fine pore structure, as the "bead" boards are merely polystyrene beads fused together.

Most adhesive manufacturers indicate on the label whether their particular formulation is satisfactory for plastic foams. Some even produce combination panel and foam adhesives that can be used on both applications. Almost all of these are very easy to use if they are designed for foam applications and will produce nearly perfect results every time.

Gypsum Drywall Adhesives

A number of the adhesive types discussed in the chapter, such as the panel adhesives, can be used to bond gypsum drywall to wood or metal studs and to laminate drywall panels (Fig. 4-7). These specially formulated adhesives greatly increase wall strength, reduce sound transmission, and improve wall appearance overall. Those made with an elastomeric base generally contain no asphalt or tar and can be painted over without fear of stain-through. A high solids content makes them an excellent gap filler that bridges irregularities. Properly applied, they stay in place without sagging and allow ample time for alignment of each drywall panel. Only minimal supplemental nailing is required on walls or ceilings, thereby reducing nail pops. As a matter of fact, many so-called "nail pops," especially on ceilings, are not really pops; the nails never move. Instead, due to the cold conditions in the attic or on outside walls, condensation forms around the nail and this condensate picks up dust and dirt. Thus, what appears as a popped nail is actually a shadow of the nailhead created by condensation. The use of gypsum drywall adhesives eliminates most nails and prevents nail shadows. It also does away with the necessity of the time-consuming job of nail patching or spackling.

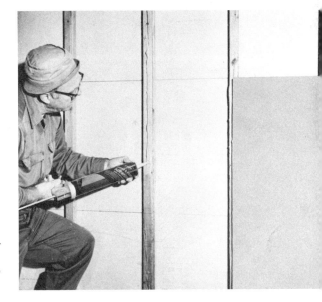

Fig. 4-7: Fewer nails are necessary to install drywall if a gypsum drywall adhesive is used to install the panels.

Other adhesives used for gypsum drywall installations are asphalt-based. Some asphalt-based products may not be suitable for gypsum drywall installations. If you have any questions, you should find out the asphalt content from your dealer and then try to determine if the product has been given an ASTM racking test, wallboard test, or any other test that would assist you in determining quality. However, should you have to use one of these products due to the lack of rubber-based systems, be absolutely sure that you do not get any smears on the face surface of the gypsum board. Asphalts have a tendency to bleed through painted surfaces and are difficult to cover with ordinary paints.

Tileboard and Wallboard Adhesives

These adhesives are specifically designed for use on large sheets of prefinished hardboard, plywood, and wallboard (Fig. 4-8). Smooth spreading and easy to use, tileboard adhesives form a high-strength bond to wood, masonry, poured concrete, plaster, and gypsum wallboard, and they are highly water resistant. (Some are even waterproof.) They usually have a working or open time of approximately 30 minutes. The open time, however, may also depend upon other variables. High ambient temperatures, low humidity conditions or dry air, and high wind conditions will all shorten the working time. On the other hand, lower temperatures and high humidity conditions or moist air will tend to lengthen the working time.

Fig. 4-8: Use a tileboard and wallboard adhesive to install large sheets of prefinished paneling.

Rubber-based or elastomeric tileboard and wallboard adhesives are very similar to the panel type already covered, except that they can be troweled rather than extruded. On trowel applications, the adhesive is normally troweled to the back of the panel over the entire surface with a V-notched spreader having notches cut a minimum of 3/16" deep, 3/16" wide, and on 5/16" centers. On prefinished hardboard applications that are being installed over existing walls or gypsum wallboard, plaster, or plywood, it is recommended that the adhesive be applied over one 4' by 8' sheet of hardboard at a time. All cutting, piecing, and trimming should be done prior to applying the mastic to the back of the panel. With warped panels or out-of-plumb wall surfaces, it may be necessary to shore or brace the panels temporarily until the adhesive has taken its initial set (usually within 6 to 8 hours). On certain applications it might be desirable to use a spot application rather than a trowel. Again, the adhesive is usually applied to the panel rather than to the wall surface. Apply the adhesive in spots or globules approximately the size of a golf ball on 12" centers. Once again, however, remember that when bonding panel to polystyrene foams you must check the compatibility of a solvent formulation with the foam.

It is not uncommon to find resin-based adhesives used on tileboard installations. These mastics are characterized by their medium brown to dark brown colors and extremely high viscosities. They are also generally quite "heavy."

These resin-based systems have a great deal of cohesive strength when wet and generally do not require any bracing of the panels while the adhesive dries. However, they do not dry as rapidly as the rubber-based systems and become rather hard and possibly brittle upon aging. This is particularly true when they are used close to hot or warm areas such as a radiator or other heat source.

For cleanup operations, commercial products available that would be suitable are mineral spirits or lighter fluid. Avoid oily-type solvents or any cleaning material that will leave an oily residue on the surface. Where the adhesive has dried, it is best to scrape off all excess with a putty knife. In some cases soaking may be necessary for several hours to completely loosen the dried adhesive. **Note:** Always make certain that the cleaning solvent used will not mar or attack the surfaces to which it is being applied by testing an out-of-the-way area. Exercise extreme caution when using flammable or toxic cleanup solvents.

Ceiling Tile Adhesives

These adhesives are specially formulated for the installation of acoustical ceiling tile (Fig. 4-9). They have ultra-high cohesive strength. *Cohesive strength* is the ability of an adhesive to adhere within itself. With ceiling tile adhesives, it is very important to have an ultra-high cohesive strength because when you install a tile on the ceiling, there is a deadweight load downward. Thus, the adhesive must remain cohesive in order to hold the ceiling tile in place without sagging. Quick green grab is another desirable trait of a ceiling tile adhesive; it must keep the tile in place without a lot of unnecessary mechanical fasteners. Sometimes the characteristics of high cohesive strength and quick grab are desired in certain wallboard installations. Because of this, some manufacturers market these adhesives as *ceiling tile and wallboard adhesives.*

Fig. 4-9: Only use adhesives with ultra-high cohesive strength to install ceiling tile.

GENERAL APPLICATION OF ADHESIVES

It has always been difficult to prepare accurate data on the coverage of adhesives because there are so many uncontrollable conditions to consider. In cartridge applications, the speed with which the extrusion is applied, how the nozzle tip is cut, the proficiency of the user, and many other factors have a decided effect on coverage. In spatula or trowel applications from metal containers, the thickness applied, the angle of the trowel, and the depth and spacing of the notches all have an influence on coverage. A cartridge or similar container has only so many cubic inches of area within its walls, so that most construction adhesives will yield similar coverages as long as the above conditions are similar and controlled. And in trowel applications it is possible to predict that, where reasonable control is exercised, you should expect to realize a minimum of approximately 40 to 60 square feet per gallon on trowel applications. Table 4-2 states the approximate coverage that can be expected by extrusion from cartridges. Most construction adhesives are available in cartridges and in pint, quart, and gallon cans.

Table 4-2: Coverage of Extrusion from Cartridges			
Volume Extruded	**Length of Bead Extruded with Various Bead Diameters**		
	1/8"	**1/4"**	**3/8"**
1 U.S. Gallon (128 fluid ounces)	1,569'	392'	174'
Large size cartridge (29 fluid ounces)	355'	89'	39'
Tenth size cartridge (11 fluid ounces)	135'	34'	15'

Note: Since the above data is calculated on the basis of cubic measurements as related to fluid measurements, these figures will provide a reasonably accurate measure of volume required for most any mastic adhesive or sealant.

The following are general instructions for the application of construction adhesive (detailed instructions for use in specific applications are given later in this book).

1. Remove dust and other foreign matter from surfaces to be bonded.
2. There are two types of installations, depending upon the type of wall surface with which you are working.
    a. Studs, joists, or furring strips—Apply the proper bead (1/8" to 3/8") as determined by surfaces to be bonded (1/8" where there is contact, 1/4" for most applications, and 3/8" for bridging gaps and where the surface is irregular). A spaghetti or serpentine pattern is recommended for large contact areas, generally on 12' to 16' centers.
    b. Existing walls of plywood, plaster, plasterboard, etc.—Solid backing walls of this type generally present the best surfaces for wallcovering materials. In this case, trowelable grade construction or tileboard adhesives should be used and the adhesive should be troweled over the entire wallcovering surface with the recommended notched spreader.
3. Apply adhesive to one surface only.
4. Press substrates firmly in order to wet the total area to be bonded. Adhesive should spread to the edges of the desired contact area.
5. Use supplemental fasteners or weight to hold substrates in position until adhesive sets.

For cleanup, commercial products available that would be recommended are mineral spirits or lighter fluid. Avoid oily-type solvents or any cleaning material that will leave an oily residue on the surface. Where the adhesive has dried, it is best to scrape all excess off with a putty knife. In some cases, soaking may be necessary for several hours to completely loosen the dried adhesive. **Note:** Always make certain that the solvent used will not mar or attack the surfaces to which it is being applied by testing an out-of-the-way area. Avoid applying solvents to polystyrene insulation. Also, use extreme caution, as many solvents are highly flammable or combustible. Provide ventilation when using solvents in a confined area. Read and heed all precautions on the label.

You should understand that many insulation and weatherproofing products can be successfully installed with adhesives, even though the adhesive manufacturer may not specifically list that application for its product. To become an expert in the use of adhesives for weatherizing simply take the time to understand which adhesives work best with certain materials. Purchase the most suitable kind of adhesive, and use it, as stated previously, in accordance with the guidelines given in this book and also, in accordance with the manufacturer's specific directions.

Flooring Adhesives

Cracks in floors—especially those in the attic floor and between the basement and first floor—are major sources of heat loss. Sometimes it is necessary to lay new flooring materials—wood parquet, planks, strips, or finger blocks—or wall-to-wall carpeting—or one of the new resilient floor coverings. Flooring adhesives (Fig. 4-10) will be of great help in making these installations.

Fig. 4-10: Some of the more common flooring adhesives that can be of help when installing energy saving floor products.

Subfloor adhesives are excellent for laying attic subfloor. They are designed specifically for bonding plywood sub-flooring directly to floor joists, but also can provide exceptional bonds to concrete, gypsum wallboard, insulation board, and similar construction surfaces. Their high degree of initial tack allows light pieces to be bonded with only momentary pressure. The allowable open time is regulated by temperature, humidity, and air circulation and the ability of the substrate to absorb solvent from the system. Irregularities and voids in substrates, such as those in wood framing members, are easily leveled with subfloor adhesive, providing a more solid back-up surface.

When selecting a subfloor adhesive, be sure that it meets all of the requirements of the American Plywood Association (APA) Specification AFG-01 and HUD/FHA Use of Materials Bulletin #60. Clean up with mineral spirits, or in small applications, with lighter fluid. Where excess adhesive has already dried, scrape with a putty knife; in some cases, soaking may be necessary for several hours to completely loosen the dried adhesive. **Note:** Always make certain that any cleanup solvent used will not mar or attack the surfaces to which it is applied by testing first in an out-of-the-way area.

Floor tile adhesives are another multipurpose category: They are water-resistant after completely drying; they are suitable for vinyl tile, vinyl asbestos tile, vinyl roll goods, rubber tile, asphalt tile, and carpeting; and in addition, they may be used on floor surfaces such as plywood and particleboard, and on smooth, dry concrete either below, on, or above grade, providing that there is no moisture or hydrostatic pressure in the floor. Most floor tile adhesives permit adjustment of the flooring material after they are applied.

So-called "fast dry" resilient floor adhesives dry quite rapidly into a "semi-pressure-sensitive" state. The dry film remains transparent so that chalk marks or other guide lines can easily be seen. It may be used on most floor surfaces such as plywood, particleboard, hardboard, and smooth, dry concrete (above, on, or below grade), again providing there is no moisture or hydrostatic pressure in the floor.

Most resilient floor adhesives are easy to clean up. Wet adhesive on the face of the tile may be removed with warm soapy water. If the adhesive has already set, remove it with a soapy steel wool pad.

Cove base adhesives are resin base formulations designed specifically for the easy installation of rubber and vinyl cove base materials. They develop excellent adhesion on wall surfaces such as plaster, gypsum wallboard, wall papers, plywood and hardboard paneling, ceramic tile, tileboard, etc.

Wood floor mastics are the products specially designed for the installation of wood flooring. They may be applied over smooth, dry concrete, plywood, particleboard, or hardboard surfaces. Remember, when choosing an adhesive, that wood floors are not compatible with emulsion systems because wood absorbs the water, causing excessive contraction, expansion, and warping.

In addition to the flooring adhesives, the general or multipurpose construction adhesives described earlier in this chapter also are suitable for flooring applications. Choose the material that meets your needs—setting time, bonding ability, and water resistance—and follow the manufacturer's directions and general application instructions given here.

Types of Caulks and Sealants 5

Sealing the many kinds of cracks and openings in your home is no small task. It takes a good caulk to plug the leaks and keep them plugged for years to come. Cracks differ in their dimensions and exposure, and can exist in many different materials; each kind of crack or opening is different and requires a particular caulk with specific characteristics.

For example, silicone is a very effective sealant. It will stick to just about any substrate—except concrete—for 20 years or more. Although silicone sealants last a long time when used under the proper conditions, they are not a good choice for sealing a foundation. Besides, why fill a crack in your foundation with a $6.00 tube of sealant when a $2.50 tube of concrete sealer will do the job better? Costs can vary greatly, and a little research and planning can get the job done right at the best possible price.

For another example, consider latex caulks. Latex caulks are excellent crack fillers where they are protected from the elements, but it would be a waste of time and money to apply them to seal gutters and downspouts. So before rushing out to purchase your caulking supply, read this chapter carefully to learn which caulks work well for the jobs you have in mind. A little time spent now can save plenty of time, labor, and money later.

CHOOSING THE RIGHT CAULK

There are several factors that should be considered when choosing a caulk for a specific application.

Form

The type of crack or gap you are trying to seal will determine the form to use. The most popular form is the cartridge, a cylindrical container that fits inside a standard caulking gun (Fig. 5-1). The gun is used to force caulk out of the cartridge through a nozzle. Caulks formulated for special applications are often sold in 6 to 8 ounce tubes. Bathtub sealing compounds are often sold in this form. The caulk is squeezed from the tube just as you squeeze a tube of toothpaste. Caulk may also be purchased in rope form. Rope caulk comes in rolls; it is soft enough to be pressed into cracks. Rope caulk is useful for sealing large crevices and hard-to-reach areas, but usually has a life-span of only one or two years.

Fig. 5-1: Caulking is simplified by using a caulking gun to extrude caulk from a cartridge.

Sealant is also available in a spray can of urethane foam. The urethane foam can be used to seal openings up to 2″ in diameter. The foam spray degrades rapidly if exposed to weather; but, for interior applications, such as in cracks around pipe openings in the basement, it performs very well.

Cost

Do not waste money on caulks that will not perform satisfactorily. A low-cost oil-based caulk will do fine for non-permanent interior applications where the caulks are not subjected to joint movement, ultraviolet radiation, precipitation, and temperature extremes. These same caulks, though, will be a waste of money on exterior applications where expansion and contraction of the substrate and weather conditions will destroy the seal. Instead, purchase high-performance sealants that will perform satisfactorily for years. Not only will you save money, but you will save time as well. As with most construction materials, the price usually reflects the quality, and you get what you pay for.

Service Life

The service lives of caulking materials vary with the quality of their manufacture. Quality, and hence durability, varies from one manufacturer to another. Some brands of caulk or sealant come with warranties that ensure service lives of from 90 days to 20 years or more.

Typical Colors

Many caulks are available in a wide range of colors. In addition to the standard white, gray, and black, caulks are available in green, brown, red, orange, etc. One manufacturer produces an acrylic latex caulk available in 12 different colors. If none of these colors coordinate with your decor, choose a clear sealant that will be unnoticeable. If all else fails to satisfy, most caulks can be painted. Do not count on a perfect color match with colored caulks; they are designed only to coordinate with their background, and to prevent sharp color contrasts.

Resistance

When choosing caulk for any application, be sure it is able to resist destructive influences. Four of these are weather related: ultraviolet light, oxidation, moisture, and water immersion. Two other destructive factors—abrasion and fire— also must be considered when choosing sealants for various applications.

Maximum Joint Width

Carefully match sealant with the size of crack that must be sealed. Oil-based caulks should only be used to seal cracks no more than 1/16" to 1/8" wide. Acrylic latex and butyl rubber caulks may be used to seal cracks 3/8" to 1/2" wide. Cracks wider than 1/2" should be filled with an SBR sealant or silicone. Urethane foam can be used to seal openings up to 2" in diameter. The alternative to using a high-grade sealant to seal large openings is to reduce the diameter of the opening with shims or trim pieces.

Drying Time

The time in which a sealant cures involves two distinct time periods. The *tack-free time* is the length of time it takes for the surface of the caulk to dry or skin over. The skin will prevent dust and dirt from collecting on the caulk. Many caulks can be painted once they are tack-free. Curing continues until the process halts and the sealant is completely stable. The amount of time the complete process takes is referred to as the *total cure time*. Surface drying time is an important consideration when the sealant must be painted soon after application and when the sealant must cure before being subjected to precipitation. Do not apply a slow-drying sealant outside when a rainstorm is imminent. The precipitation may cause the sealant to bleed and stain the substrate. Carefully read the label for such warnings.

Flexibility

Joints between dissimilar materials, such as the junction of a chimney and the siding, must be sealed with a flexible sealant. The differing rates of thermal expansion subject the sealant to mechanical stresses that will destroy a low-performance caulk. Choose a sealant with good weathering characteristics that can be compressed and stretched without failing.

Adhesion and Cohesion

A caulk that sticks well to a substrate has good *adhesion*. It will not easily pull away. A caulk that sticks together well has good *cohesion*. It will not pull apart. Obviously, a sealant that is high in both properties is an excellent choice for stress joints.

PURCHASING SEALANTS AND CAULKS

Once you have determined the kinds of caulking materials that will be needed to seal the cracks in your house, choose a reputable manufacturer. Check labels for warranties and compliance with federal regulations. Buy quality instead of economy. Properly sealing a house takes a generous part of a weekend. Unless you enjoy caulking, it is advisable to buy a quality product with a proven performance record and one that will last for years.

After inspecting your home for cracks and points of air infiltration, how do you know how much caulking to purchase? The information in Table 5-1 should enable you to arrive at a close estimate of the amount of caulking you will need. If you do not wish to measure the number, length, width, and depth of the cracks in your house, estimate your caulking needs with this standard rule of thumb: The average house will need one-half cartridge per window or door, four cartridges for the foundation sill, and two cartridges for a two-story chimney. Buy enough caulking to finish the job. Usually retailers will allow you to return unused cartridges. If your caulking needs warrant it, buy a whole case. You can save 20% to 40% of the single tube price by purchasing full cartons (12 to 24 cartridges).

Table 5-1: Caulk Coverage per Cartridge
(Approximate linear feet)

Bead depth	Bead width				
	1/8"	1/4"	3/8"	1/2"	3/4"
1/8"	96	48	32	24	16
1/4"	48	24	16	12	8
3/8"	32	16	11	8	5

"CAULKPLEXITY"

Literally hundreds of brand name caulks and sealants have flooded the market, but most of these are variations of the formulations given in Table 5-2. Caulking is a simple operation; its most difficult aspect is "caulkplexity," or simply knowing which sealant to purchase from this bewildering assortment. There is more misinformation about caulking than correct information. Therefore, the following sections describe in depth the six generic types of sealants readily available to the homeowner. These six sealants will seal nearly every energy-leaking crack and opening in your home. By the time you reach the end of this chapter, much of the caulkplexity, or confusion associated with selecting caulks and sealants, will be gone.

Oil-Based Caulks

The oil-based caulking compounds were the first sealants to be used commercially and still account for a large percentage of sealing in residential construction, remodeling, and repair. Compared to the newer elastomeric sealants, the oil-based sealants are relatively simple substances. They consist of an oil (fish, soybean, tung, castor, etc.), a bulking filler such as clay, and additives that impart special properties to the caulk (for example, increased tackiness). Oil-based caulks dry or cure slowly so that the sealant remains flexible for a year or more.

The oil-based caulks usually have a very low initial cost. Unfortunately, many formulations available have very short life spans and tend to develop cracks within a year or so. Oil-based caulks also lack the adhesion of some of the elastomeric caulks, since they tend to become brittle and hard. They are not intended to be elastic materials and should never be used in working joints. Because they are oil-based, these caulks tend to "bleed" while drying. For this reason, allow oil-based caulks to cure 24 hours before painting over them. Oil-based caulks are recommended only for temporary sealing and gap filling on wood, metal, and plastic surfaces. As a class, they are the lowest in quality of any caulks on the market.

Butyl Rubber and Rubber-Based Caulks

The growth of butyl rubber began during World War II when natural rubber was scarce. In the 1950s, the first butyl rubber caulks were introduced in the construction industry and have since become widely used. Butyl rubber caulks (Fig. 5-2) are very good from a sealing standpoint. They have excellent water resistance, and they adhere to a wide variety of surfaces. Butyl rubber is versatile enough in its properties for it to be packaged and sold as "Gutter and Downspout Sealer," "Driveway Crack Sealer," "Concrete Block Sealer," and other specialty products.

However, butyl rubber caulks have several potential disadvantages. Most are quite stringy and difficult to apply. They also tend to remain tacky and collect dirt. They require at least 12 to 24 hours, and may take up to three to seven days of cure time before they can be painted. This varies with each manufacturer. Generally, butyl rubber caulks are priced in the same range as the acrylic latex caulks.

Fig. 5-2: Butyl rubber and other rubber-based caulks are long lasting and have superior resistance to water.

	Sealant	Special Uses	Durability (years)	Adhesion	Shrinkage Resistance
Basic performance	oil and resin caulks	glazing	1 to 2	fair to good	poor
	polybutene cord or rope	very wide gaps	1 to 2	none	excellent
Intermediate performance	nonacrylic latex; PVA	indoor and protected surfaces	2 to 5	good, except to metal	fair
	acrylic latex	indoor and protected surfaces	10 to 20	excellent, except to metal	good
	butyl rubber	metal to masonry	7 to 10	excellent	fair
	butadiene styrene (SBR)	anywhere	15 to 20	excellent	excellent
	neoprene	concrete	15 to 20	excellent	good
High performance	polysulfide	anywhere	20 or more	excellent	excellent
	polyure- thane	anywhere	20 or more	excellent	excellent
	silicone	anywhere	20 or more	good, excellent with primer	excellent

Table 5-2: Characteristics of Caulks and Sealants

Butyl rubber caulks are satisfactory for most construction surfaces and are ideal for gutter and downspout use (Fig. 5-3) or for similar areas that are exposed frequently to moisture. Do not use butyl rubber caulks where they will be subjected to lengthy immersion. They are also not recommended for decorative or painted surfaces where appearance is a consideration. Cleanup must be done with paint thinner or naphtha.

There are also premium grade rubber-based adhesive caulks that offer maximum performance on wood, metal, masonry, glass and other construction materials. These flexible, long-lasting caulks are highly weather-resistant.

Latex Caulks

Latex caulks have achieved popularity along with latex paints. The relationship is obvious: Whereas the oil-based caulks will often bleed through a latex paint, leaving an unsightly color streak, the latex caulks are compatible with the latex paint system and produce a smooth-looking finish. The name "latex caulks" covers many different materials; but, in general, these materials have one of two

Tack-free (hours)	Cure (days)	Cleaner	Primer	Paint
Table 5-2: Characteristics of Caulks and Sealants (Continued)				
24 to 48	up to 1 month	paint thinner	needed on porous surfaces	should be painted
remains permanently moist and pliant		no cleaning required	none needed	should not be painted
1/4 to 1/2	1 to 3	water	none needed	optional
1/4 to 1/2	1 to 3	water	needed on porous surfaces	optional
up to 30 days	15 to 30	paint thinner	none needed	optional
1/2 to 2	1 to 3	naphtha, paint thinner	none needed	optional
1	3 to 4	toluene, xylene, MEK	none needed	optional
24 to 72	7	toluene, TCE, MEK	neoprene primer is needed	optional
24	4 to 14	acetone, MEK, paint thinner	none needed	optional
1	2 to 5	naphtha, toluol, xylol, paint thinner	follow manufacturer's instructions	follow manufacturer's instructions

Fig. 5-3: Butyl rubber is ideal for sealing gutters and downspouts. In fact, butyl caulks are often called "gutter seals." They are usually available in either white or gray.

bases: vinyl acrylic or polyvinyl acetate (PVA). The acrylic is quite similar to the acrylic latex used in the manufacture of paint, and the polyvinyl acetate is similar in structure to the white glues sold as household adhesives. Both have their distinct advantages, but the vinyl acrylic caulks (generally referred to as acrylic latex caulks) are on the whole somewhat superior to the non-acrylic latex caulks with a PVA base.

PVA Latex Caulks.   Polyvinyl acetate latex caulks (Fig. 5-4) are of a better quality than most oil-based caulks. They are easier to use and do not have the disadvantage of a slow curing time. Unfortunately, some manufacturers have chosen to load their latex caulks with fillers that result in lower-grade products with questionable long-term sealing characteristics. Those in the lower price ranges generally do not perform much better than the oil-based caulks.

Fig. 5-4: Non-acrylic latex caulks are inexpensive and have a life span of several years.

Non-acrylic latex caulks are recommended primarily for interior surfaces, but can be used to seal exterior surfaces other than concrete and cement. Latex caulks will tolerate a great deal of intermittent water exposure but should not be immersed. Do not choose this type of caulk for areas such as gutters and downspouts. In other exterior applications, apply a coat of paint to increase the caulk's ability to tolerate rain. Latex caulks tend to lose their adhesive quality under moderate joint expansion; so, they should not be used on expansion joints. All non-acrylic latex caulks are fast drying. They are generally tack-free in less than an hour, and can then be painted with latex- or oil-based paints.

These caulks are easy to apply, last as long as 2 to 5 years, and clean up easily with water. Some have fairly good adhesive strength and can be used for household bonding such as sticking loose wall tile back in place or gluing non-stress joints in wood.

Acrylic Latex Caulks.   The use of acrylic latex caulks (Fig. 5-5) has increased faster than that of any other type of caulk. This increase is due to a number of significant advantages, including ease of application, long life (up to 20 years),

Fig. 5-5: Acrylic latex caulks are one of the best all-around sealants available to the homeowner and have life expectancies of about 20 years.

fast drying time, and simple cleanup. Acrylic latex caulks dry to a tack-free finish and can be painted minutes after being applied. These caulks can also be manufactured in an almost endless variety of colors. Highly weather-resistant acrylic latex caulks normally cost slightly more than oil-based or straight latex-based caulks.

Disadvantages are few and slight. Acrylic latex caulks should not be applied when temperatures are below freezing and, although they will bond to wet surfaces, these caulks should not be applied if there is a threat of rain within the next 12 to 24 hours. Their slightly higher cost is more than offset by their superior performance and long life.

Acrylic latex caulks can be used on virtually any residential or small commercial caulking application where better than usual sealing performance is desired over a long period of time. When you plan to protect and preserve your home for many years, this is the first caulking material to select. Acrylic latex caulks are also available in a variety of colors for use with painted and stained siding. A color-coordinated application eliminates any unsightly contrast of colors and the need for touch-up painting.

Butadiene Styrene (SBR) Sealants

Another sealant recently introduced to the homeowner is the butadiene styrene or solvent-based rubber (SBR) sealants. Made with a high percentage of polymers, SBR sealants (Fig. 5-6) adhere exceptionally well to virtually all building materials. They provide superior adhesion on glass, metal, brick, stone, masonry, ceramics, fiberglass, concrete, wood, and most painted surfaces. SBR sealants also stretch readily. Tests have shown that they will stretch 200% to 250% before failing. Because of their unique adhesive and cohesive properties, they can be used on mobile homes, automobiles, trucks, and travel trailers for sealing windows, door edges, and trunk moldings.

Fig. 5-6: SBR sealants are excellent for expansion joints between dissimilar materials
such as masonry and siding.

SBR sealants are highly weather resistant. They are very resistant to ultraviolet radiation; thus, they can be used to seal windows (Fig. 5-7) and skylights.
They are also very resistant to moisture and can be used on chimney flashing,
gutters, and downspouts. SBR sealants should not be used, however, for joints
that are immersed in water, such as in swimming pools.

The SBR sealants can be produced in a wide range of colors. Some formulators
produce a clear sealant that goes on clear right from the tube. The better quality
clear sealants will not turn gray, chalky, or "cloudy" as they age. Most SBR
sealants can be painted over with oil-based or latex paints; solid color stains; or
other wood, metal, or masonry overcoat products. Unlike some siliconized products, they will not reject paints or coating. Cleanup can be accomplished with a
solvent.

Fig. 5-7: A clear SBR sealant is ideal
for sealing windows.

Silicone Caulks

The best-known high-performance elastomeric caulks are the silicone sealants (Fig. 5-8). They also have excellent working properties. Uncured, they are very soft and very easy to extrude from a caulking gun. Temperature has little or no effect on the gunning characteristics of the sealant. It can be extruded over a temperature range of -40°F to over 200°F. Cure, of course, is retarded by cold weather; therefore, installation should be avoided during low temperatures.

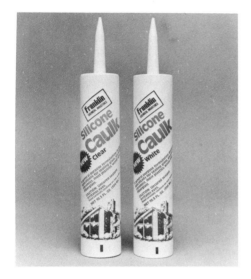

Fig. 5-8: Silicone sealants are extremely long-lasting with many excellent sealing characteristics.

Silicone sealants also adhere well to most surfaces and materials, but surfaces must be cleaned thoroughly before the sealant is applied. Some silicone sealants also require priming of the joint before application. Always follow the manufacturer's instructions in regard to priming.

The most outstanding property of the silicone sealants is high elongation recovery. Specimens compressed and held for one year may show as much as 98% recovery upon removal of the load. Silicone sealants also have an excellent resistance to weathering. They are unaffected by moisture, ultraviolet radiation, and reactive forms of oxygen in the atmosphere. Consequently, they have a long life span—well over 20 years.

Obviously, silicone caulking products are considered to be one of the best caulks available; however, they are usually quite expensive, often costing up to two to three times as much as other caulks. Because silicone caulking products are so expensive, they are usually best reserved for specialized jobs as opposed to general household caulking. On exterior applications, better results can normally be obtained on a more economical basis by utilizing a high-quality acrylic latex caulk or SBR rubber caulk. Although some manufacturers now have silicone caulks that can be painted, most of these caulking products cannot be painted. Once the caulk has been applied, cleanup can be accomplished with naphtha or paint thinner.

Partially used cartridges can be stored for future use without worry that the sealant in the cartridge will solidify. Simply force a little bit of the silicone into the plastic tip of the cartridge, then let it cure. This plug of cured sealant effectively closes the opening. To reuse the cartridge, remove the small plug of cured material.

Glazing Compounds

A glazing compound is used to hold window panes in place and seal off air infiltration between the glass and frame. Glazing compounds bond tightly to glass, wood, and metal surfaces. Latex-based glazing formulations (Fig. 5-9) have greater adhesion and are more durable than those that are oil-based; they resist cracking, stay flexible, and can be used on damp surfaces for indoor and outdoor applications. Latex compounds dry in as little as 30 minutes and can be painted with either oil- or latex-based paints. Glazing compounds should not be applied when air or surface temperatures are lower than 45°F.

Fig. 5-9: Glazing compound for sealing glass panes.

Special Purpose Sealants

There are a variety of other sealants, putties, mortars, and caulks that you will find helpful. Most of these are variations of the sealants and caulks described earlier in the chapter. They are marketed for use in specific applications such as sealing tubs, concrete, blacktop, roofs, windows, etc. (Fig. 5-10). Usually, these sealants are formulated with special additives that adapt the sealant to the application. If you have a special caulking need, such as sealing the edge of a tub or sealing cracks in a masonry foundation, use one of the special purpose sealants. There will then be no question as to whether or not you have matched the right caulk with a specific application.

Fig. 5-10: Caulks and sealants are formulated into specialty products such as concrete sealer, asphalt sealer, and tub and tile caulk.

Tub and tile caulks are specifically designed for permanent water-tight seals around tubs, sinks, showers, lavatories, and other ceramic, metal, and plastic surfaces. In addition to cartridges, most tub and tile caulks are available in 6 ounce squeezable tubes for easy application. Before setting, tub and tile caulk should be smoothed with a wet finger or putty knife. Cleanup can be accomplished with warm, soapy water. These caulks will dry white, and will not crack, peel, or mildew.

Blacktop repair caulks are excellent for filling and sealing cracks in blacktop driveways, for sealing loose shingle tabs, roof seams, gable joints, and metal building seams, and to stop leaks in flashing and around vent pipes, downspouts, and gutters. Blacktop repair caulks are tough and flexible and dry to a textured finish to match most asphalt and roof surfaces.

Concrete repair caulks are other special purpose sealants that can be used for repairing cracks in sidewalks and patios, brick walls, driveways, and other masonry areas, and to prevent air and moisture entry and ice damage.

Concrete patch, or concrete adhesive, as it is sometimes called, comes in two basic types: One is an acrylic system and the other a polyvinyl acetate system. The acrylics are much more waterproof and should be used on all exterior applications.

Concrete patch caulks make it possible to bond new wet stucco, plaster, or cement mixes to old concrete, stone, wood, metal, and other similar surfaces. Before applying, be certain that the surfaces are clean and free from dust, dirt, and loose materials. It is not, however, necessary to do any keying or joint raking. Spread the concrete patch—using a brush, spray gun, or roller—over the entire surface to be repaired in much the same manner as you would paint.

Concrete patch can also be used to impart extra strength to portland cement mixes (Fig. 5-11), and to level uneven floors of concrete, wood, old tile, or other

Fig. 5-11: Versatile concrete patch can even be added as a fortifier to a concrete mix.

surfaces prior to the installation of new flooring materials. To use the patch for leveling, mix it in the same proportions as you would for using it as a fortifier. Apply the mix to the old surface with a trowel and then smooth it to a level finish. The mix may be troweled from a featheredge to a thickness of 2". Cracks and voids in the subfloor surface can also be filled and troweled smooth.

CARTRIDGE GUNS

Cartridge guns are the most common means of applying energy-saving adhesives and caulks. While the use of the cartridge gun is explained in the next chapter, it should be mentioned here that it is wise to buy a sturdy, all-metal type. When selecting a gun, make sure that it has a ratchet-controlled plunger, and that it can be turned easily to relieve extrusion pressure. Most guns are available in standard cartridge sizes (Fig. 5-12).

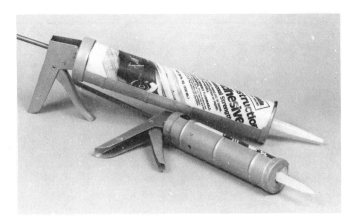

Fig. 5-12: Cartridge guns are usually available to handle two standard cartridges: the 10-1/2 ounce size and the 29 ounce size.

Sealing Your House with Caulks 6

Your home energy audit undoubtedly discovered numerous cracks and crannies through which cold winter air could enter your house. Finding them was the hard part. Now that you know where air infiltration is occurring, it is a simple matter to fill the openings with caulk. In fact, caulking appears to be such a simple task that it is very easy to do it poorly. And an inferior caulking job, regardless of the quality of sealant used, will be ineffective in stopping air infiltration. So, pay close attention to the preparations and methods of application suggested in this chapter. Properly done, a weekend spent caulking and sealing your home should keep your house weathertight for years.

THE IMPORTANCE OF CAULKING

Caulking accomplishes more than the elimination of infiltrating air. It also helps stop water penetration into the home. Water penetrating through walls and roofs can have several detrimental effects, including the corrosion of metal construction components and the decaying of wood framing and finishing materials. The presence of moisture will also reduce the effectiveness of most fibrous insulating materials. As the tiny air spaces in the insulation become filled with water, the insulating value of the material decreases.

Weatherproofing your home with caulking has additional advantages. Reducing air infiltration also reduces airborne sound, and a home that is soundproof has a snug, sheltered feeling that contributes to your comfort. Caulking also covers up unsightly construction defects at places such as the junction of siding and window frames. Cracks and crevices are also entry ports for destructive insects and vermin. Mice and rats may seek refuge within walls and between floors; snakes may slip into a basement in search of food; stinging insects may build large nests in an attic or behind exterior siding if they somehow gain entrance. Insects that reside in wood focus their attack on damp wood, especially in crawl spaces and around the foundation. Some of these problems are merely annoying, but natural intruders can also take a devastating toll. For instance, termites—only one of the many insects that are capable of disintegrating wooden structures—cost American homeowners upward of a half billion dollars each year in damage repairs or in fees for professional exterminators. Therefore, sealing potential entranceways and controlling moisture are very important in overall house protection.

TOOLS AND MATERIALS

The various types of caulks and sealants used to eliminate air infiltration are described in detail in Chapter 5, so you should refer to this information when selecting the correct caulking for the job. In addition to the caulk and caulking gun, you will need several other inexpensive, readily available tools and materials to do the job correctly.

Have a good ladder or solid stepladder on hand to help reach high places. A putty knife or large screwdriver, wire and fiber brushes, and turpentine are also needed to help clean the areas to be caulked. For larger cracks and openings, oakum, glass filler strips, or some other suitable filler material will be needed to plug most of the opening.

APPLICATION OF CAULK FROM A CARTRIDGE

Caulking cartridges are designed to fit a standard caulking gun that pushes caulking out of the cartridge and into a crack with a trigger-activated plunger.

To load a caulking gun, first turn the plunger rod so that the plunger teeth are facing up, and then pull the plunger rod as far back as it will go (Fig. 6-1A). Next, insert the caulking cartridge in the top opening and press the nozzle of the caulking product firmly into the slot at the front end of the gun. Then, turn the plunger rod so that the metal teeth face down, and engage the trigger mechanism (Fig. 6-1B).

After the cartridge has been loaded, snip off the sealed tip of the nozzle at a 45° angle. Do not cut through the nozzle too near the end; the bead (the flow of sealant) will be too small. Do not cut too close to the cartridge, either; the bead will be difficult to control, and the application will be messy. Trim the nozzle so that the size of the opening is slightly smaller than the smallest gap to be filled (Fig. 6-1C). Some cartridges have nozzles marked with bead widths, such as 5/8" or 1/4", which make it easy to determine where the nozzle should be cut.

A foil or plastic membrane seals the caulk in the cartridge. This must be punctured before the caulk will flow into the nozzle. Push an extra long nail or a stiff piece of wire down the nozzle (Fig. 6-1D). Jab several times through the membrane so that the caulk will discharge easily. The size of bead can be controlled as shown in Fig. 6-2.

Surface Preparation

Before caulking, make sure the area to be caulked is properly prepared. Clean the area thoroughly. Remove old sealant and chipped paint with a putty knife or large screwdriver. Wipe the crack with a brush dipped in turpentine to get rid of any remaining dirt and debris.

Use of the Gun

After the cleanup has been accomplished, practice using the gun before actually filling a crack. Make a few trial strokes on a piece of old lumber to

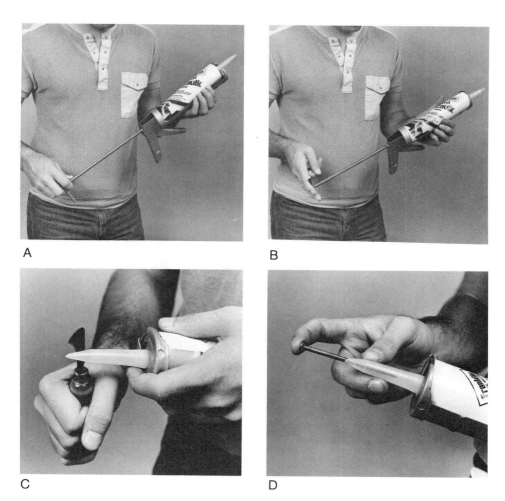

Fig. 6-1: To prepare the cartridge for caulking: (A) Pull the plunger back as far as possible, insert the cartridge, and (B) turn the plunger teeth down. (C) Slice the tip of the cartridge off at a 45° angle. (D) Puncture the membrane with a long nail.

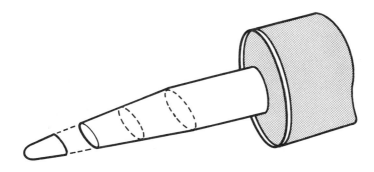

Fig. 6-2: The size of the bead can be controlled by the way the tube nozzle is cut. The more that is cut from the tip of the nozzle, the larger the bead.

achieve a smooth flow of sealant. If you desire a very exact bead or if the surface is porous and hard to clean, outline the caulking area with masking tape (Fig. 6-3). When the tape is removed after depositing the bead of caulk, you will have a clean, straight edge. Be sure you remove the tape before the caulk begins to set; removing the tape after the caulk begins to harden may pull the caulk away from the gap.

To apply the caulk, hold the gun at a 45° angle to the surface and squeeze the trigger with a steady pressure. As the caulk begins to flow, push the gun along the crack as rapidly as needed to force an even bead of sealant into the crack (Fig. 6-4).

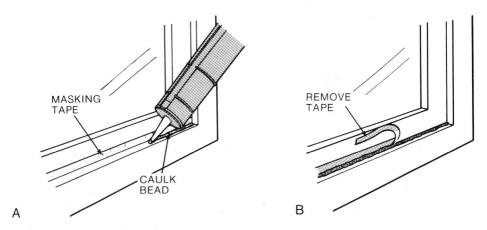

Fig. 6-3: (A) By outlining the sealing area with tape, (B) you can be sure of a nice, straight edge.

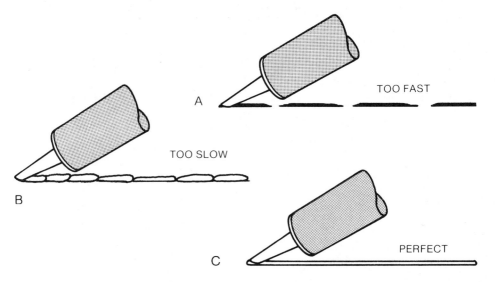

Fig. 6-4: (A) Moving too quickly will leave voids in the caulk. (B) Moving too slowly will pile the caulk up into ugly ripples. (C) Moving at a steady speed will produce an even, consistent bead of caulk.

APPLICATION OF CAULK IN ROPE FORM AND TUBES

Rope-type caulking products are very easy to apply. This material is usually used for temporary seals and hard-to-reach corners. Rope caulks can be used in single or multiple strands, depending on the size of the crack. Simply unroll the product and, with fingers or a putty knife, press the caulk into the crack (Fig. 6-5). If fingers are used instead of a knife, wetting the fingers will make them less likely to stick to the sealant.

Caulks in roll-up tube containers are usually reserved for small areas such as around outside water faucets and vents. To use, simply snip off the top of the nozzle in the same way the top is cut off the caulking cartridge. Apply the caulking by squeezing the tube from the bottom just as if you were squeezing a tube of toothpaste. Push the tube slowly across the crack, sealing up the entire area (Fig. 6-6). Unlike cartridges, tubes of caulk often have a cap that can be replaced on a partially used tube to prevent the unused portion from hardening.

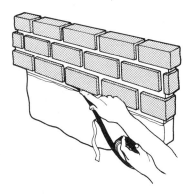

Fig. 6-5: Firmly press rope caulking into place.

Fig. 6-6: Sealing with a squeeze-tube of caulk does not require a caulking gun. Replacing the tip will preserve the caulk.

TIPS FOR CAULKING

Here are some tips that will make any caulking job go smoothly:

1. Never apply any caulking product when the temperature is below 45°F unless the manufacturer's instructions permit it. On cool days, the caulking will be easier to work with if it is warmed before being used (placed in a warm oven, perhaps). Similarly, on hot summer days, caulking can get hot and soft. Chill the cartridge in the refrigerator for an hour or so to firm it up.

2. Prepare to caulk by cleaning the area to be caulked. Pry away defective caulking with a putty knife or old screwdriver. Brush away all loose material and dirt. Clean the surface with turpentine. Use a primer if required with the caulk you are using.

3. Regardless of the type of caulking product used, caulking is not recommended for cracks over 1/2" deep. If a larger crack needs filling, first plug the space with oakum, wood, cotton, or fiberglass insulation. Fill to within 1/2" of the surface. Then, apply one or more beads of caulking over the filling material until the gap is sealed.

4. Many caulks are flammable—do not smoke when applying these products.

5. Start in an inconspicuous place. Fill small cracks first; then, enlarge the tip opening and fill larger cracks.

6. Hold the gun at a 45° angle, keep a consistent pressure on the trigger, and push the gun along the crack. Pulling caulk over a crack merely lays a bead of caulk down on top of the crack. The product should be *pushed* deep into the crack (Fig. 6-7).

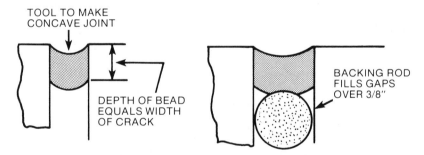

Fig. 6-7: Push the caulk deep into the crack, rather than just laying a bead of caulk on top of the crack.

7. Do not move too quickly; you will leave gaps in the bead. Do not move too slowly, either; the bead will pile up in ripples. Maintain a constant, even speed.

8. Wipe the nozzle often and turn the handle to release pressure after each run.

9. Moisten your finger and smooth each bead. Do this immediately before the bead can begin to harden.

10. Plug the used cartridge to keep it fresh until it is needed again. Reversing the point of the tip that was cut off will provide a good plug.

11. Painting after curing will improve the life of most caulks. Check the manufacturer's instructions for paintability and curing time.

TIPS FOR SPECIFIC CAULKING JOBS

The following sections supply additional information for weatherproofing your home with caulks and sealants.

Doors and Windows. Doors and windows are good places to begin any home caulking project. Every window and door fills a large hole in your home, and a crack runs around each one where it fits into the house frame. You can see why doors and windows deserve special attention.

Clean all areas, and prefill large cracks if necessary. Use a color-coordinated acrylic latex caulk on both interior and exterior surfaces in order to avoid unsightly color contrast or the need to paint over the caulk (Fig. 6-8). Seal any loose windows and glazing with a clear acrylic or silicone sealant. Door thresholds must also be sealed. Remove the threshold, extrude an acrylic latex caulk along its underside, and replace it (Fig. 6-9).

Fig. 6-8: Seal around window frames and doorframes with color-coordinated acrylic latex caulk.

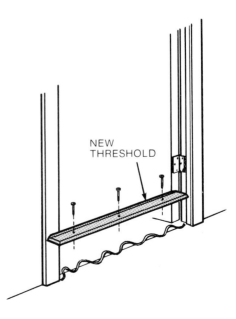

NEW THRESHOLD

Fig. 6-9: Apply caulk to the underside of the threshold to seal out infiltration.

Siding Junctions.   Several different caulks should be used to seal the joints of various building materials. A butyl rubber sealant should be used to seal cracks and joints in flashing and gutters. A color-coordinated acrylic latex should be used to seal joints where separate sections of siding meet. Expansion joints between dissimilar materials should be sealed with a high-quality sealant such as an acrylic, rubber, or silicone sealant (Fig. 6-10). Prefill deep gaps with a filler before caulking. Painting over these areas after caulking will protect sealants from weathering and ultraviolet radiation.

Fig. 6-10: Expansion joints should be filled with a high-quality sealant.

Masonry and Foundations.   Fill cracks in masonry walls and foundations (Fig. 6-11) with an acrylic latex caulk, a butyl rubber caulk, an acrylic concrete sealant, or a cement patching compound. Scrape away any loose masonry or mortar and prefill before sealing. Feather the edges of the caulk over the edges of the cracks.

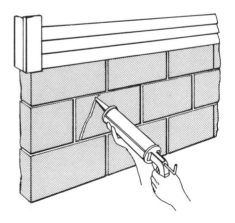

Fig. 6-11: Cracks in masonry must also be sealed to keep out wind and water.

Pipe and Wire Penetrations.   Openings for pipes, electrical wires, antenna cables, and telephone cables should not be ignored however small they may be. Seal around pipes with butyl rubber (Fig. 6-12) and around wires with acrylic latex (Fig. 6-13). If possible, turn off the electricity before caulking around electrical wiring. Do not overlook drainage pipes and wiring that pass through the floor of your house. For example, the drainage pipe for your bathtub is only accessible from the basement or crawl space below. Stuff the openings for such pipes with filler material and seal with an acrylic latex or butyl rubber caulk. For hard-to-reach areas, use rope caulk, pressing it into place with a long screwdriver.

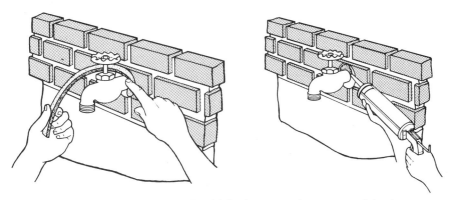

Fig. 6-12: Seal the opening through which pipes pass into or out of the house.

Fig. 6-13: Wire entries must also be sealed.

Baseboards.   Baseboards require a little more work than most other caulking jobs; therefore, use a high-quality acrylic latex caulk so that the seal will last for years. Carefully pry the baseboards away from the wall (Fig. 6-14A), and pull the carpet away from the wall to protect it from soiling (Fig. 6-14B). Stuff the gap between floor and wall finish with fiberglass (Fig. 6-14C). Caulk the gap between the floor and the wall (Fig. 6-14D), and replace the carpet and baseboard (Fig. 6-14E).

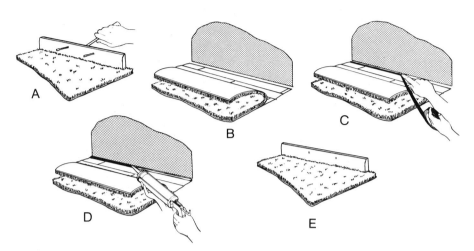

Fig. 6-14: (A) Remove the baseboard and (B) fold carpet away from the wall. (C) Fill large gaps with fiberglass. (D) Fill the crack with acrylic latex caulk. (E) Replace the carpet and baseboard.

Electrical Outlets and Switches.   Electrical outlets and switches also require some mechanical work before sealing. First, turn off the electricity. Then, remove the plates that cover the switches and outlets. Purchase gaskets designed to seal such openings and cut to size (Fig. 6-15). Fit the gaskets over the outlet or switch and replace the covers. Wall outlets can be further sealed by placing plug covers in unused outlets.

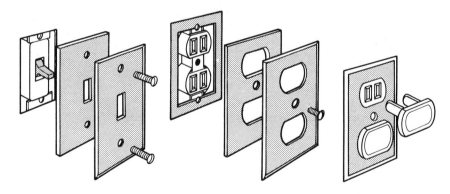

Fig. 6-15: Gaskets are specially designed to seal electrical outlets and switches.

Sole Plate.   An acrylic latex caulk should be used between the sole plate and the foundation (Fig. 6-16). Before caulking, clean debris and old caulk from the area, and fill large gaps to within 1/2" of the surface with a filler material. In homes with a full basement, it may be easier to seal the sole plate from inside if the lower course of siding covers the plate.

Vents and Exhaust Fans.   A vent that passes through a wall to the outside may be a direct route for infiltrating air. Remove the interior vent cover and cut a

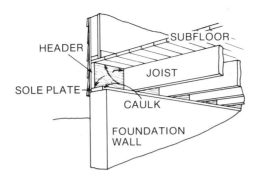

Fig. 6-16: Prefill large gaps with fiberglass, and caulk any cracks adjacent to the sole plate.

piece of plastic to fit over the inside of the cover. Push the plastic and vent cover back into place and trim off any excess plastic protruding around the vent cover. Seal the edge of the vent with a clear acrylic or silicone caulk. Be sure to remove the plastic when warm weather returns.

Exhaust fans in the kitchen, bathroom, and laundry are vented to the outside. The edges of the vent covers should be sealed with an acrylic latex caulk. Make sure that the vent closes completely when the fan is not in operation. Dryer vents are notorious for standing open.

Tubs, Showers, Sinks, and Toilets. Bathroom, kitchen, and laundry fixtures are areas where moisture could leak into wall and cabinet areas. The edges of these fixtures should be sealed with a special tub and tile sealant or with a clear acrylic or silicone sealant. Seal the tub and shower where they meet the wall and floor (Fig. 6-17A). Seal around all faucets and the shower head (Fig. 6-17B). Seal around the edge of the kitchen, bathroom, and laundry sinks (Fig. 6-17C). Seal the base of the toilet where the toilet rests on the floor (Fig. 6-17D).

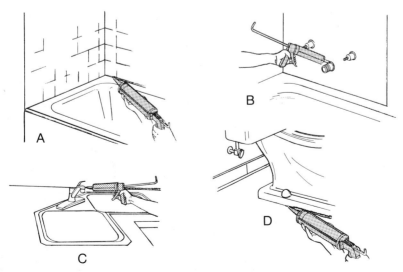

Fig. 6-17: Caulk around the edge of (A) tubs and showers, (B) faucets and shower heads, (C) sinks and countertops, and (D) toilets.

Window Glazing.   Window glazing compounds hold and seal the glass in window frames. Since glazing compounds are subjected to sunlight, fluctuating temperatures, rain, and other destructive factors, their periodic renewal is necessary. The first step in a glazing renewal procedure is to remove the old, cracked glazing compound by scraping with a putty knife or similar scraping tool (Fig. 6-18A). A propane torch or heat gun may help to soften the tough, dry material, but be sure to shield the glass from the heat.

When reglazing windows, it is not necessary to remove the glazier's points or the glass pane, but make certain that all dust and glazing debris has been removed from the area before beginning to apply the new glazing compound (Fig. 6-18B). After the surface has been properly prepared, dip the new glazing compound out of the container, using a putty knife or glazier's tool, and distribute it along the edge of the glass, forcing it into the sash (Fig. 6-18C). Fill the L-shaped recess between glass and frame completely, and use the V-shaped end of the glazing tool to form a 45° angle between the glass and frame (Fig. 6-18D). Use the edge of the knife to cut a clean line against the window (Fig. 6-18E). Paint the area after the compound has dried.

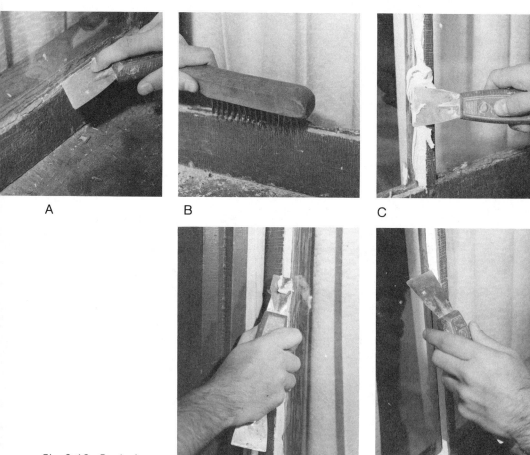

A   B   C

Fig. 6-18: Reglazing a windowpane.   D   E

Weatherstripping Materials 7

The average American house has an assortment of windows and doors, each requiring a particular type of weatherstripping to properly seal out infiltration. Quickly make a mental survey of your house. How many double-hung windows, casement windows, sliding windows, awning windows, stationary windows, jalousie windows, etc., do you find? In addition to its several entrance doors, does your house also have sliding glass doors, French patio doors, a garage door, an attic hatch, a pet entrance door, or a mail slot? Each of these windows and doors requires careful attention regarding the choice of weatherstripping products. There are almost 30 generic types of weatherstripping from which to choose, and the variations of materials, methods of attachment, size, and shape make the selection very large indeed. Not one of the different kinds is suitable for every situation, although some are much more versatile than others. Many have been developed for specific applications (such as for casement windows and garage doors). Choosing the best weatherstripping for each window and door may be confusing unless you are fully acquainted with the materials available.

Table 7-1 lists some of the most common types of weatherstripping and describes the advantages or disadvantages of each one.

COMPRESSION GASKETS

Compression gaskets (Fig. 7-1) form the largest single category of weatherstripping materials. As the name implies, compression gaskets are designed to be squeezed between two surfaces. They are made of soft, spongy materials that conform to even or slightly irregular surfaces when compressed. Compression gaskets are made in a variety of application types.

Felt Strips

One of the least expensive weatherstripping materials is felt (preshrunk wool felt is better than hair felt). Felt is available in plain strips or hemmed with aluminum (Fig. 7-1A). An aluminum backing gives the felt more body and increases its sealing ability. Felt is commonly used to seal even surfaces such as door jambs and the top and bottom of double-hung windows.

Table 7-1: Weatherstripping Characteristics and Comparisons

Material		Cost	Ease of Application	Method of Attachment	Suitable for Nonuniform Surface	Quality of Seal	Life Expec-tancy (years)	Notes
felt	wool, preshrunk hair	low	easy	nails, staples, glue	no	fair	1-3	unsightly; damages easily
plastic foam tape	plastic, vinyl, rubber	low	easy	glue, self-adhesive	yes	fair	1-3	should not be painted
wood strips edged with foam	plastic, vinyl	low	moderate	nails, glue	no	good	1-3	will not stand friction
rolled tubular gasket	plastic, vinyl	moderate	moderate-difficult	nails, staples, glue	yes	good	2-5	loses flexi-bility at 20°F
foam-filled tubular gasket	plastic, vinyl	moderate-high	moderate-difficult	nails, staples, glue	yes	very good	3-6	good for exterior applications
casement window gasket	plastic, vinyl	moderate	easy	glue	no	good	10	metal casement windows only
spring metal	brass, bronzed, aluminum	moderate-high	moderate	nails	no	excellent	20	many applications

Table 7-1: Weatherstripping Characteristics and Comparisons (Continued)

	Material	Cost	Ease of Application	Method of Attachment	Suitable for Nonuniform Surface	Quality of Seal	Life Expectancy (years)	Notes
door sweeps	vinyl, felt	low-high	moderate-difficult	screws	no	good	N/A	adjustable
threshold gaskets	vinyl gasket, wood or metal threshold	very high	difficult	screws	no	very good	N/A	vinyl insert is replaceable
interlocking metal	aluminum, steel	high-very high	difficult	screws	no	excellent	20	requires periodic maintenance
magnetic	steel magnets and holders in plastic housing	moderate-high	difficult	nails, staples, glue	no	excellent	N/A	complex mounting
astragal	vinyl	moderate-high	moderate	nails, screws	no	good	N/A	requires careful fitting

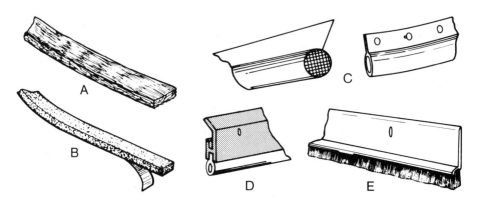

Fig. 7-1: Compression gaskets: (A) felt strips, (B) foam strips, (C) tubular gaskets (open and foam-filled), (D) tubular gasket with an aluminum flange, and (E) bristle weatherstripping.

Foam Strips

Plastic foam strips (Fig. 7-1B) are also inexpensive and are one of the easiest forms of weatherstripping to install. Usually the foam strip has an adhesive backing that eliminates the need for nails or tacks. Foam strips are also available attached to wood nailers. *Open-cell* foam is made from polyurethane and is the least expensive. *Closed-cell* foam is made from vinyl and, although vinyl costs more, it is more durable than polyurethane.

Tubular Gaskets

A commonly used weatherstripping that has more versatility than foam or felt is the tubular gasket (Fig. 7-1C). Tubular gaskets are available in several variations. There are hollow vinyl tubes or tubes filled with polyurethane foam. Tubular gaskets are equipped with vinyl nailing flanges, some of which are reinforced with an aluminum hem (Fig. 7-1D). The tubing can be tacked into place or may be purchased with an adhesive backing. Regardless of the type you purchase, tubing can be bought in 17' lengths that will completely seal a standard door jamb. Correctly installed, the tubing will press against the closed door or window, sealing off the gaps.

Bristle Weatherstripping

Aluminum doors and windows are often factory-equipped with bristle weatherstripping—short, dense, brush-like fibers protruding from a U-shaped metal backing (Fig. 7-1E).

TENSION STRIPS

Tension strips (Fig. 7-2) are one of the best choices of weatherstripping for many different applications. They are long strips of thin metal or plastic that are

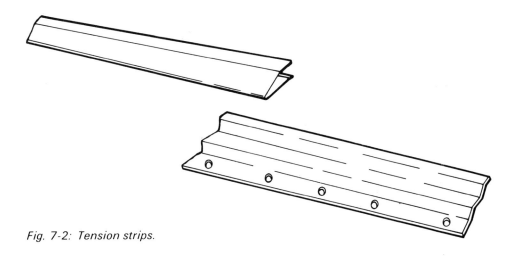

Fig. 7-2: Tension strips.

bent into V or L shapes. When compressed between two surfaces, the V or L exerts tension on the surfaces as the metal tries to spring back into place (thus, the popular name "spring metal"). The tension assures that the weatherstripping will fit tightly against the mating surfaces, effectively sealing out air infiltration.

SPECIALTY WEATHERSTRIPPING

Some weatherstripping products are designed for a particular application. If possible, use one of these types whenever applicable. Specialty weatherstripping products are generally more expensive than the more versatile types of weatherstripping, but they seal out air infiltration better and generally last longer.

Casement Window Gaskets

Casement windows are best weatherstripped with a special casement window gasket (Fig. 7-3). This sponge rubber gasket has a groove that slips over the lip of a casement window sash. The gasket is glued in place and should perform well for many years.

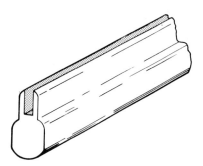

Fig. 7-3: Casement window gasket.

Door Sweeps

Door sweeps (Fig. 7-4A) are designed to seal the bottom edge of a door. They are basically a flexible vinyl or bristle flap attached to a rigid flange or retainer. The flange is screwed to the base of the door and the flap extends down to seal the gap between the door bottom and the threshold.

Threshold Gaskets

A worn wooden threshold can be replaced with an aluminum threshold that is equipped with a threshold gasket (Fig. 7-4B). The gasket is made of soft vinyl and bulges upward to create a friction fit with the bottom edge of the door. When worn, the gasket can be replaced. Gaskets of various sizes are available to seal doors that swing over average, thick pile, or shag rugs.

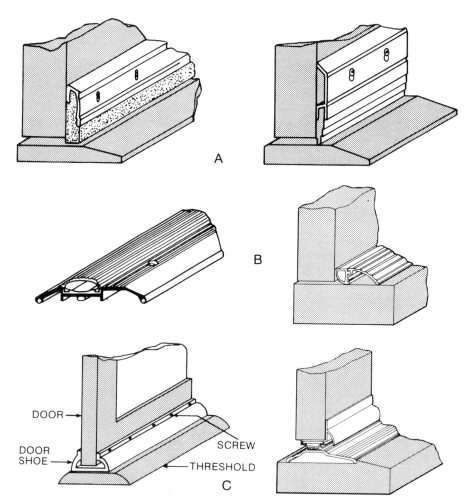

Fig. 7-4: (A) Vinyl door sweep. (B) Aluminum threshold gasket with vinyl insert. (C) Garage door shoe.

Door Shoes

Strips of heavy sponge rubber or rubber tubing are also designed to seal garage doors (Fig. 7-4C). Nailed or screwed to the bottom of the door, the shoe presses tightly against the garage floor when the door is shut. The sponge rubber shoe has enough compressibility to seal uneven floor surfaces.

Magnetic Weatherstripping

Sliding patio doors and sliding windows can be sealed with magnetic weatherstripping (Fig. 7-5). This type of weatherstripping is much like the magnetic gaskets on a refrigerator door. It comes in two parts: a long powerful strip magnet encased in a specialized, flexible gasket and a metal strip. The metal strip is mounted to the door or window, and the magnetic gasket is mounted to the frame. When the door or window is closed, the magnet seals itself to the metal strip.

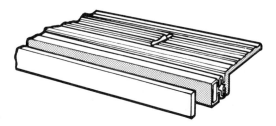

Fig. 7-5: Magnetic weatherstripping.

Astragal Weatherstripping

French doors and double doors can be sealed with astragal weatherstripping (Fig. 7-6). This type of weatherstripping is in the shape of a T. On one side of the T is attached a flexible lip or bulb. When the T is properly attached to one of the halves of a double door, the compressible gasket will seal tightly against the other half of the double door when both doors are closed.

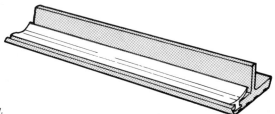

Fig. 7-6: Astragal weatherstripping.

Interlocking Metal Strips

One of the most effective forms of weatherstripping is interlocking metal strips (Fig. 7-7). The strips are two interlocking precision-formed metal sections that fit together like a jigsaw puzzle. These also create a very tight seal for sliding doors.

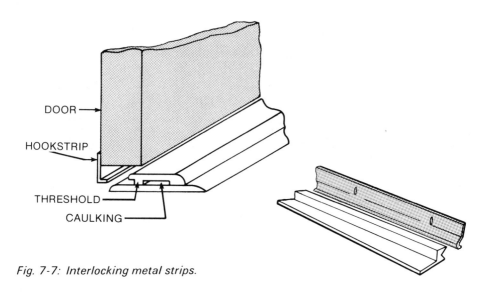

DOOR →

HOOKSTRIP

THRESHOLD

CAULKING

Fig. 7-7: Interlocking metal strips.

In selecting your weatherstripping, make sure you have the right kind for the job you want to accomplish. If after reading this and the next chapter you still have any doubts or questions, ask the salesperson at your local hardware store or home center for advice, so that you do not come home with exactly what you did not want or need.

PURCHASING WEATHERSTRIPPING

The types of weatherstripping materials mentioned in this chapter can be found at your local hardware store or home center. Some types are available in kits that include all the necessary hardware.

To find the total length of weatherstripping needed, measure the window or door frame accurately. Make a complete list of how many strips of each length are required for all the windows and doors to be weatherstripped. Then, purchase the correct kits, or simply add up and buy the total amount of weatherstripping needed and cut to correct lengths when installing.

To obtain best results from a weatherstripping installation, don't limit yourself to the obvious locations, such as windows and doors that lead outside, but also consider such spots as unheated spare rooms, doors that lead to unheated areas such as sunporches, basements, attics, crawlspaces, garages, etc., dryer vents, and unusual "windows" such as skylights. It is important to keep in mind that weatherstripping is *not* a substitute for storm windows and storm doors. (In fact, it is a good idea to weatherstrip them, too.)

Weatherstripping Windows and Doors 8

Most energy loss by infiltration occurs through and around windows and doors. The best solution to infiltration is weatherstripping. Table 8-1 is a list of 17 different areas that require weatherstripping. Specific weatherstripping products are suggested for each application. Those categories that are starred indicate the best match-up of application and material. The chart is not meant to be exhaustive or restrictive. Other match-ups of applications and materials are also possible. The key ingredient in any weatherstripping task is not the product, but the care with which the material is applied. Sloppily installed, the best weatherstripping material will be a waste of money. If out-of-plumb windows and warped doorframes are not repaired, no material will properly seal out infiltration. On the other hand, the most simple weatherstripping product, if installed with care on doors and windows in good repair, will stop infiltration. Success or failure primarily depends on you.

WEATHERSTRIPPING DOORS

Doors are a major source of air infiltration. Unlike windows, they cannot be shut or sealed off for the winter, and every time someone opens a door, cold outside air and warm inside air change places. The goal of weatherstripping doors is to prevent any exchange of heat for cold air while the door is shut. Entrance doors, attic doors, garage doors, pet doors, and mail slots should be carefully sealed to minimize heat loss.

Sealing with Felt or Foam Strips

One inexpensive way to weatherstrip a door is with felt or foam strips. If applied carefully, these compression gaskets will provide a good, temporary seal. The strips can be purchased in 17' lengths, which contain enough material to seal one standard doorframe. Felt strips can be attached with either aliphatic resin glue, white glue, or tacks. Foam strips often have a self-adhesive binder.

To install felt or foam strips with tacks, cut the strips into three lengths—two equal to the height of the doorframe and one equal to the width. Next, extrude a narrow bead of acrylic latex caulk to the back side of the strips. The caulk will seal between the weatherstripping and the doorframe, and will act as a glue. Finally,

Table 8-1: Applications of Weatherstripping

Types of Weatherstripping	Doors										Windows						
	Standard sides	Standard bottom	double (Dutch)	sliding	ext. basement	attic hatch	storm	garage	pet doors	mail slots	standard (double-hung)	Casement metal	Casement wood	horizontal slide	awning	non-opening	storm
Compression Gaskets																	
Felt strip	✓					✓				✓						✓	✓
Open-cell foam			✓		✓	✓			✓	✓							★
Closed-cell foam			✓		✓	★	✓			✓			★		✓	★	★
Sponge rubber	✓				✓	✓										✓	
Gasket and flange		✓						✓	★		✓	✓		✓		✓	✓
Reinforced gasket and flange	✓	✓					★	✓				✓					
Bristle				★			★							✓			
Tension Strips																	
Metal	★		★	✓	★	✓	✓		✓	✓	★	★	✓	★	★	✓	✓
Plastic	✓			✓							★	✓	✓	✓	✓		

Table 8-1: Applications of Weatherstripping (Continued)

	Applications																
	Doors										**Windows**						
	Standard		double (Dutch)	sliding	ext. basement	attic hatch	storm	garage	pet doors	mail slots	standard (double-hung)	Casement metal	Casement wood	horizontal slide	awning	non-opening	storm
Types of Weatherstripping	sides	bottom															
Specialty Designs																	
Door sweep		★						★									
Threshold gasket		✓															
Magnetic									★								
Interlocking			✓														
Astragal			✓														
Comments Key		A		B		C		D									B, C

★ Best solution.
✓ Suitable solution.

(A) Treat bottom same as standard door.
(B) If possible, renew factory-installed weatherstripping first.
(C) Seal with duct tape if hatch is infrequently used.
(D) Bottom only.

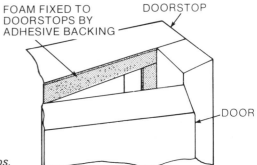

Fig. 8-1: Nail felt strips to the doorstops.

tack the strip to the exterior side of the doorstops (Fig. 8-1). Do not tack the strips to the door itself where the weatherstripping will run the greater risk of being bumped and damaged. When the door is closed, the felt should be compressed between the door and the stop.

Sealing with Tubular Gaskets

Tubular gasket type weatherstripping—either hollow or foam-filled—is easy to install. It may be attached to either the doorstop or to the door itself. Properly installed tubular gaskets will provide a very good seal, but if heavy traffic will subject the gaskets to the probability of being bumped and torn loose, use another type of weatherstripping.

Cut the tubular gasket into three lengths—two for the side of the door and one for the top. If using weatherstripping with a metal hem, file off any burrs after cutting the strips to the proper length.

If applying the gasket to the doorstop, position the gasket so that it protrudes over the edge of the stop (Fig. 8-2A). When the door is shut, the gasket will press tightly against it. To attach weatherstripping to the door instead of to the door-stop, close the door and position the strip so that the vinyl or foam gasket presses against the doorstop (Fig. 8-2B). Then, nail or tack the stripping to the door. Be sure that there is continuous contact around the door.

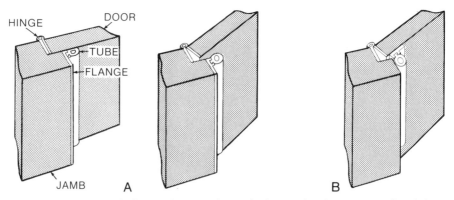

Fig. 8-2: (A) Attach tubular gasket weatherstripping to the doorstop so that it is com-pressed when the door is shut; (B) tubular gasket weatherstripping can also be attached to the door.

Sealing with Tension Strips

The most popular type of weatherstripping used to seal doors is spring metal tension strips. Spring metal tension strips provide an excellent seal on doors that are not warped or out of plumb. They are easily installed (Fig. 8-3), and the tight seal they provide will last for years.

The first step in the installation of spring metal tension strips is to carefully measure for the four individual pieces of spring metal that are needed to weatherstrip the door. Measure from the threshold to the bottom of the striker plate, and from the top of the striker plate to the top jamb. Cut two pieces to these dimensions. Measure and cut a piece to fit from threshold to top jamb on the hinge side of the door. Finally, measure and cut stripping for the top jamb above the door. Cut a 1/8" taper on each end of the top strip so that it will not interfere with the side strips.

Most spring metal strips are installed with nails and have prepunched nail holes. When nailing, avoid striking the metal with the hammer. Instead of driving the nails completely flush with the metal with a hammer, drive the last 1/8" of each nail with a nail set or a large nail.

Often, spring metal weatherstripping kits include a lock strip. The lock strip seals the area in front of the lock where spring metal cannot be installed. This is the first piece that should be installed. Then, install the two strips above and below the striker plate; file off any burrs, and position the strips so that the nailing edges face the door. Leave a 1/8" gap between the free edge of the strip and the doorstop. Finish the door by installing the strips on the opposite side jamb and the top jamb.

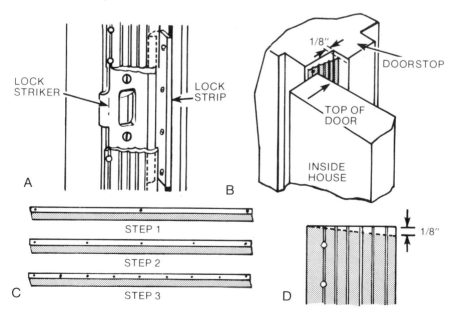

Fig. 8-3: To weatherstrip a door with spring metal tension strips: (A) Install the lock strip and the tension strips above and below the lock striker; (B) install the side pieces 1/8" below the top jamb; (C) nail in the pattern shown; and (D) cut a 1/8" taper on both ends of the head strip before nailing.

Installing Door Sweeps

The simplest way to seal off cold air passing under a door is to install a door sweep (Fig. 8-4). In most cases, the sweep retainer will have elongated screw slots so that the sweep can be adjusted to the proper height. As the vinyl or bristle strip wears from use, the screws can be loosened and the sweep lowered to compensate for the wear.

To install a door sweep, close the door, measure the width, and cut the sweep to fit. Hold the strip in position with the bottom edge touching the floor, and then mark screw hole locations in the door at the bottom of the elongated slots. Start the hole with an awl or ice pick and drill the holes for the two outside screws. Attach the strip to the door with these two screws. Check the strip for proper sealing when the door is shut and for proper clearance over the floor when the door is open, adjusting the height as necessary. Drill the other holes and drive the screws. Again, check for proper sealing and clearance and then tighten the screws.

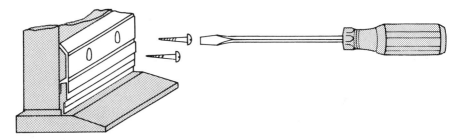

Fig. 8-4: Position the door sweep and place the screw at the bottom of the elongated slot.

Installing Threshold Gaskets

A well-designed threshold probably provides the best seal against cold air passing under a door. It is wise to replace any door thresholds that are badly worn. A new metal threshold, with a vinyl gasket providing a very good seal beneath the door, is a good replacement choice. Follow these steps in replacing a worn threshold.

1. Fasten cardboard around the threshold to protect the floor or carpet.

2. Attempt to remove the old threshold with a pry bar. If it does not lift up easily, cut through each end of the threshold and then force up the center piece (Fig. 8-5A).

3. Tap out the remaining ends of the threshold with a hammer and chisel (Fig. 8-5B). If the new threshold is higher than the old, it will be necessary to saw through the doorstops to enlarge the opening to the new threshold height.

4. Thoroughly clean the sill with turpentine.

5. Cut the threshold to fit tightly against both sides of the doorframe. Extrude a bead of acrylic latex, butyl or butadiene styrene caulking under it.

6. Position the threshold so that the flap side of the plastic seal is toward the outdoors. Lift up the flap and insert screws through the holes in the strip underneath (Fig. 8-5C).

7. Remove the door and cut a slight taper in the door bottom so that a tight seal is formed when the door is shut.

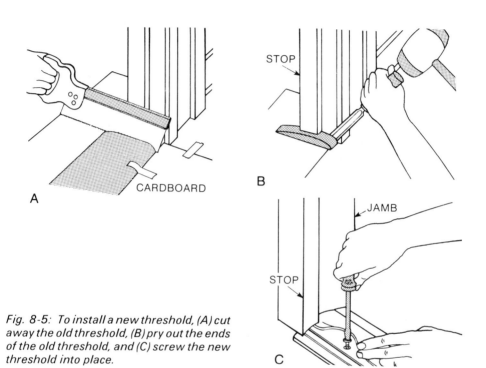

Fig. 8-5: To install a new threshold, (A) cut away the old threshold, (B) pry out the ends of the old threshold, and (C) screw the new threshold into place.

Sealing Garage Doors

Garage doors which when closed do not rest flush against the driveway can be a major source of air infiltration. Providing a tight seal to reduce this infiltration will keep the garage warmer and reduce heat loss from the heated rooms adjoining the garage.

The finest means of attaining this tight seal is to screw or nail heavy-duty rubber gaskets to the bottom of a garage door. Prior to installation, make sure the bottom of the garage door is in good condition. A fresh coat of paint will increase the door's resistance to moisture. When installing the gasket (Fig. 8-6), open the door so the bottom edge is accessible and prop it fast with a suitable piece of lumber. Apply the weatherstripping so that the thickened edge of the channel is on the outside of the door and fasten the material in place with heavy nails or screws. The weatherstripping should have enough resiliency to adjust to the irregularities of the driveway and provide a tight seal.

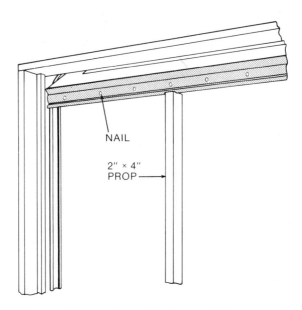

Fig. 8-6: Nail the heavy rubber gasket to the bottom of the garage door.

WEATHERSTRIPPING WINDOWS

Although windows normally are sealed much more tightly than doors, they cannot be overlooked when tightening your house against air infiltration. Unless your windows are sealed with interlocking metal flanges between sash and frame, inspect each window for worn-out weatherstripping. Because the total window area of a house is usually far greater than the total exterior door area, weatherstripping windows can be a major task. Therefore, choose a quality weatherstripping to avoid having to repeat the job every one or two years.

Sealing Double-Hung and Sliding Windows

Several types of window weatherstripping can be used to seal double-hung windows. The same is true of horizontal sliding windows, which operate in much the same way as double-hung windows. Felt and foam strips are the least expensive and easiest to install, but both will tear if used between moving parts. Felt will attract dirt and can only be used on interior surfaces, and it also is difficult to install. Vinyl, if applied to exterior surfaces, may pull away in cold weather or stick during warm weather. Probably the best choice for weatherstripping windows is spring metal strips. These are durable and are hidden when the windows are shut.

Sealing with Tension Strips. On double-hung windows, tension strips are installed in the side channels of both upper and lower sashes, on the bottom rails of the upper and lower sashes, and on the top rail of the upper sash. Figure 8-7 illustrates the installation procedures.

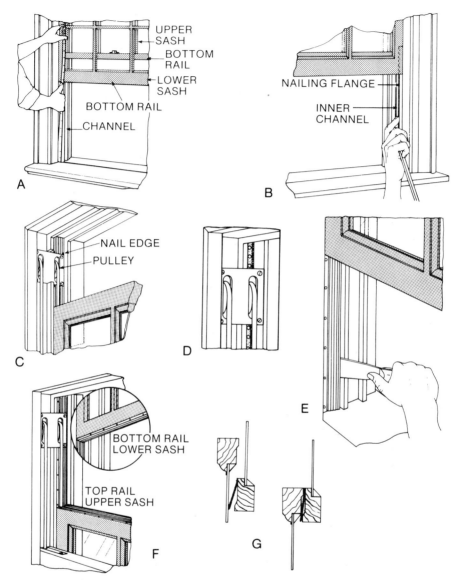

Fig. 8-7: To seal a double-hung window with spring metal tension strips, follow these steps: (A) Measure the windows for the 5' length of weatherstripping, cut the stripping to size, and bevel the ends 1/8". (B) Slip the side piece up between the sashes and the window frame. (C) If the windows have pulleys, cut a small strip to fit above the pulley and (D) tack the bottom edge of the strip to prevent the strip from interfering with the operation of the window. (E) Bow the strips out to increase the tension of the strips. (F) Attach strips to the top rail of the top sash and to the bottom rail of the bottom sash. (G) Finish the application by tacking a strip to the inside of the bottom rail of the upper sash.

Sealing with Tubular Gaskets. Another means of sealing a double-hung window is with vinyl and rubber gaskets. While weather-resistant vinyl or rubber gasket strips cannot be hidden away like tension strips, they can be applied to the outside of a window where they are not visible (Fig. 8-8).

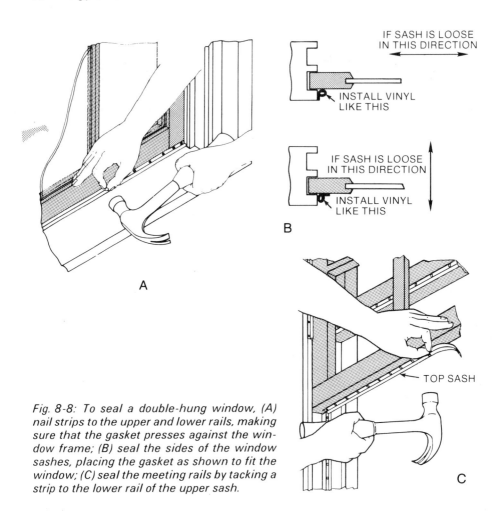

Fig. 8-8: To seal a double-hung window, (A)
nail strips to the upper and lower rails, making
sure that the gasket presses against the window frame; (B) seal the sides of the window
sashes, placing the gasket as shown to fit the
window; (C) seal the meeting rails by tacking a
strip to the lower rail of the upper sash.

Sealing with Compression Gaskets.   Foam and felt can be used to seal any
window area not subjected to friction. The upper and lower rails of a double-
hung window can be effectively sealed with either felt or foam. Cut the felt or
foam strip 1/16" shorter than the length of the window to prevent the weatherstripping from rubbing against the casing. With either glue or small tacks, attach
the strips to the underside of the lower rail and to the top of the upper rail
(Fig. 8-9).

Felt or foam can also be used to weatherstrip metal windows. Metal windows
are usually grooved around the edges so that the flanges interlock. With time,
gaps will appear, and weatherstripping should be applied. Weatherstripping that
requires mechanical fasteners is often unsuitable for metal windows. Wire
brads or screws may interfere with the operation of the window. But, felt or foam
attached with adhesives will not cause the window to bind or jam. Brushing the
metal with a wire brush, dusting, and wiping clean with solvent, will help to
attach adhesive-backed weatherstripping firmly. Do not be surprised if prepar-
ing to weatherstrip a window takes more time than actually applying the
weatherstrip.

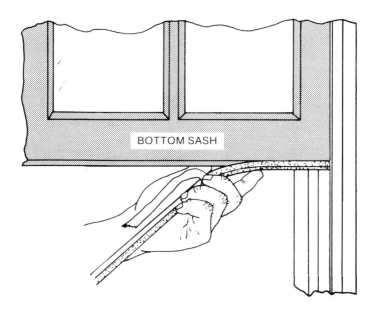

BOTTOM SASH

Fig. 8-9: Either self-adhesive foam or felt can be applied to the bottom rail of the bottom sash and the top rail of the top sash.

Weatherproofing Casement and Awning Windows

The inside perimeter of casement windows should also be weatherstripped if there is not an efficient seal. The same applies to awning windows, which are really sidewise casements. Spring metal strips are most commonly used in these cases. Cut strips to fit along all four sides of the window frame. Bevel the edges of the top and bottom strips to prevent them from interfering with the side strips (Fig. 8-10). Tack the strips onto the jamb alongside the window stops to ensure a snug fit when the window is cranked shut. For casements that open outward, the nailing flange should be placed along the outside edge of the frame. If the window opens inward, place the nailing flange on the inside edge.

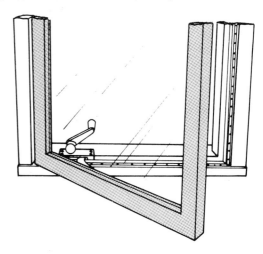

Fig. 8-10: Spring metal strips are most commonly used to weatherstrip the inside perimeter of casement windows if there is not an efficient seal.

Metal casement windows can be weatherproofed with a special casement window gasket (Fig. 8-11). This vinyl gasket has a deep groove that slips over all four edges of the frame. The gasket is applied with a special vinyl-to-metal adhesive. Follow the manufacturer's instructions for cleaning the window frame and applying the adhesive. Install the gasket so that the window closes against the flat side of the strips. If properly installed, the casement stripping should last for years.

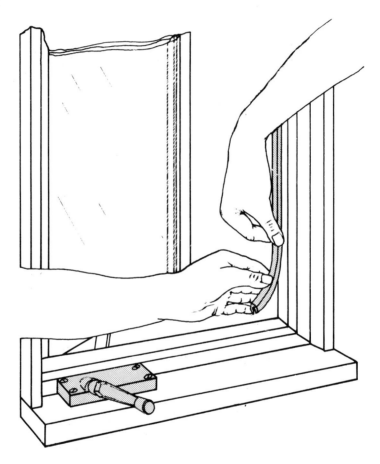

Fig. 8-11: Metal-framed casement windows are easily sealed with vinyl casement window gaskets.

Choosing and Buying Insulation 9

Once you have stopped the escapement and infiltration of heat through openings in your home with the use of caulks, sealants, and weatherstripping, it is time to consider insulating the structure. Of course, if you do not complete these weatherizing measures first, you are simply wasting your money buying insulation. But, with these priority weatherization procedures completed, however, the addition of insulation (or supplementing of existing insulation) is a fairly inexpensive and, for the most part, easy do-it-yourself task that can save you another 20% to 30% of your heating and cooling costs.

In addition to using less energy, insulation increases your comfort by reducing drafts. Walls, ceilings, and floors are warmer because the flow of air in convection currents is decreased. By retarding heat transfer, insulation has a significant influence on indoor comfort conditions and the ease with which they can be controlled. Most adults are comfortable at temperatures of 70°F to 72°F in mild weather but prefer higher temperatures during severe cold periods. The passage of radiant heat from the human body to wall, floor, and ceiling surfaces of markedly lower temperature makes it necessary for room temperatures to be raised to compensate for the loss of body heat.

Another consideration with insulation is moisture control. Moist air feels warmer than dry air at the same temperature; therefore, a moderate relative humidity is desirable within living spaces. However, movement of this moisture must be controlled through the use of vapor-resistant membranes. This controls the moisture level within the structure and helps prevent moisture from passing through the structure and condensing, possibly causing structural damage from rot. Many insulations are produced with attached vapor-resistant membranes made of foil/kraft laminate facing or a kraft facing. Unfaced insulation requires application of a separate vapor-resistant membrane such as 4 or 6 mil polyethylene film or foil-backed gypsum wallboard.

SELECTION OF AN INSULATION

Several types of insulating materials are available in several different forms. You can choose from fiberglass, rock wool, cellulose, vermiculite, perlite, polystyrene, and polyurethane—to name a few of the most common. Depending on your choice, the insulation can be installed in blankets, batts, loose-fill, rigid boards, or foam. R-values are the chief consideration, but there are other factors involved in selecting the best material for your home situation. Table 9-1 com-

Table 9-1: Comparative Properties of Insulation Materials

Materials	R-Value per Inch	Cost per R-Value	Resistance to:				Applications:							
			Fire	Water Absorption	Water Damage	Direct Sunlight	Roofs, Cathedral Ceilings	Flat Ceilings, Attic Floors	Wall Cavities	Exterior Sheathing	Floors over Unheated Spaces	Interior Masonry Walls	Exterior Masonry Walls	Exterior Foundation (below ground)
Blankets and Batts														
Fiberglass	3.2	1.3¢-1.6¢	B	B	A	A	A	A	A	D	B	C	D	D
Rock Wool	3.4	1.3¢-1.6¢	A	B	A	A	A	A	A	D	B	C	D	D
Loose-Fill														
Fiberglass	2.2	1.4¢-1.8¢	B	B	A	A	C	A	B	D	B	D	D	D
Rock Wool	2.9	1.4¢-1.8¢	A	B	A	A	C	A	B	D	B	D	D	D
Cellulose	3.7	0.9¢-1¢	C	D	D	B	C	A	B	D	C	D	D	D
Perlite	2.5	3.3¢-5.6¢	B	C	B	A	D	A	C	D	D	D	D	D
Vermiculite	2.1	5¢-6¢	B	B	B	A	D	B	D	D	D	D	D	D

Table 9-1: Comparative Properties of Insulation Materials (Continued)

Materials	R-Value per Inch	Cost per R-Value	Resistance to:				Applications:							
			Fire	Water Absorption	Water Damage	Direct Sunlight	Roofs, Cathedral Ceilings	Flat Ceilings, Attic Floors	Wall Cavities	Exterior Sheathing	Floors over Unheated Spaces	Interior Masonry Walls	Exterior Masonry Walls	Exterior Foundation (below ground)
Rigid Board														
Expanded Polystyrene	4.0	3.5¢-4.5¢	D	D	B	D	B	C	B	A	B	A	A	C
Extruded Polystyrene	5.0	6¢-8¢	D	A	A	D	B	C	C	A	B	A	A	A
Polyurethane and Poly-isocyanurate	7.1-7.7	5.5¢-8.3¢	D	B	A	D	B	C	C	A	B	A	A	A
High-Density Fiberglass	3.85-4.76	7.3¢-8.6¢	B	B	A	A	B	C	C	A	A	A	C	D
Reflective Foil														
Reflective Foil	6.4-11	3¢-5¢	N/A	A	A	A	D	D	C	D	B	D	D	D
Foamed/Sprayed in Place														
Urethane	7.1	10¢-16¢	D	A	A	D	A	C	A	D	C	A	A	C
Cellulose	3.5	11¢-23¢	C	D	C	B	D	D	D	D	D	A	A	D

A = Excellent; B = Good; C = Fair; D = Unsatisfactory; N/A = Not Available.

pares R-values, prices, properties, and suitability in various applications of the most common insulation materials. Carefully study this table and the following pages before purchasing insulation for your house.

R-Values

Insulation is rated by R-values, which are expressed as numbers, for example, R-30. As explained in Chapter 2, "R" means resistance to winter heat loss or summer heat gain. The higher the R-value, the greater the insulating power. One type or brand of insulation might be thicker or thinner than another, but if they have the same R-value, they will perform the same.

Calculating the total R-value is usually unnecessary. The Federal Trade Commission requires the total R-value rating to be printed on all blankets, batts, and boards. Loose-fill insulation has the R-value per inch printed on the bag, along with information that explains the thickness necessary to achieve various total R-values. It is important to check this information carefully before purchasing a particular type and brand of insulating material. If the insulation is not marked, do not buy that product or allow the contractor to install it. Also be wary of unsupported claims of high R-values. The authoritative guide to use is the *Handbook of Fundamentals of the American Society of Heating, Refrigerating, and Air-Conditioning Engineers* (ASHRAE), 345 E. 47th St., New York, NY 10017. Claims of R-values higher than those listed by ASHRAE should be suspect.

Other Considerations in Selecting Insulation

Remember that you need to insulate only once for the life of your home. Therefore, it is important to select the best insulation you can find and afford for the particular area to be insulated. Ideally, the insulation should possess the following characteristics:

1. An efficient barrier to the transfer of heat.
2. Nonburning.
3. Lightweight.
4. Nonsettling.
5. Odorless.
6. Vermin-resistant.
7. Immune to water vapor.
8. Rotproof and permanent.

In some cases, expense can be a consideration. If you install the insulation yourself, the only expense you will incur is the price of the insulation. Obviously, the least expensive insulation that will give you the desired R-value is often the best investment of your money. For example, fiberglass batts or blankets, though lower in R-value per inch, cost less per R-value than cellulose, board, and foam insulations. Not only are they relatively inexpensive, but they are easy to install in unfinished walls, floors, ceilings, and attics.

Of course, if the insulation is installed professionally, you must consider the installation cost as well as the cost of the insulation. You will save money by doing as much of the installation as possible by yourself—for example, removing siding or boring holes to permit installation of cellulose or foam.

On the other hand, the least expensive is not always the most practical from the standpoint of ease of application. For example, fiberglass batts cannot be placed in finished walls without removing interior walls. The practical alternative is to blow cellulose or foam insulation into the walls. This cost-application principle may also apply when insulating your basement. Bonding polystyrene boards directly to masonry walls with an adhesive may be less costly and less time consuming than constructing a frame wall to receive fiberglass blankets or batts. The situation often dictates your choice of material.

Batts or Blankets

Batts or blankets are flexible materials composed of felted fibers of mineral wool (Fig. 9-1). Mineral wool is a generic term that includes fiberglass and rock wool. Mineral wool blankets and batts are the least expensive type of insulation and are among the easiest to install. Because they are very resilient, a number of them can be compressed into a single, heavy kraft bag. Packaging in this way makes storage and handling much easier. When the bags are opened and the insulation has a chance to "breathe," the batts or blankets will expand back to their original size.

Fig. 9-1: Typical batts and blankets.

Fiberglass. This product consists of long filaments of spun glass that are loosely felted and cut into batts or blankets of different widths (15" and 23") and thicknesses ranging from 3-1/2" to 12". The fibers are coated with phenolic resins to provide bonding between the fibers. Batts are either covered with an asphalt-laminated kraft paper or have a foil vapor barrier on one side with a flange on each edge for stapling to joists or studs (Fig. 9-2). They may also be unfaced and are usually designed for friction-fit (Fig. 9-3).

Fiberglass itself is an inorganic, noncombustible material. Organic binders, used in the production of batts and blowing wool, are flammable. Facings on fiberglass building insulation usually consist of an asphalt-coated kraft or foil-faced paper laminate, which are both flammable. When installed, the facing must not be left exposed.

Fig. 9-2: Blanket stapled to a wall.

Fig. 9-3: Blanket held in place by friction.

Advantages. Fiberglass has a reasonable cost/R-value; it is easy to install, relatively nonflammable, resistant to water damage, nonsettling, and suitable for many uses.

Disadvantages. It cannot be installed in enclosed cavities and may be irritating to skin and *upper respiratory tract.* **Note:** When working with blankets and batts of fiberglass insulation, it is recommended that you wear a mask, although it is not a safety precaution according to all manufacturers.

Rock Wool. This material is similar to fiberglass, except the raw material used to produce it is steel, copper, lead, or naturally occurring rock.

Since it is usually made from rock or slag and is melted at temperatures above 2,192°F, the base material of batts or blowing wool is noncombustible. Binders added to it may be flammable. Asphalt-coated or foil-laminated kraft paper may be used as a vapor barrier facing on these batts and should also be considered flammable. It should be covered by gypsum board or other fire-retardant materials.

Advantages. Rock wool insulation is similar to fiberglass; the R-value, however, is about 10% greater.

Disadvantages. It cannot be installed in enclosed cavities; batts are damaged easily during handling.

Loose-Fill

Loose-fill insulation (Fig. 9-4) is manufactured from a wide variety of materials and may be installed by either blowing or pouring. If loose-fill materials are blown, they should be applied at the specific density designated by the manufacturer.

All loose-fill insulations have the advantage of filling irregular horizontal spaces easily.

Fiberglass. Loose-fill fiberglass insulation has the following advantages and disadvantages:

Advantages. It has a reasonable cost/R-value; is relatively nonflammable; is resistant to water damage; and can be blown or poured.

Disadvantages. It has low R-value/inch; may settle after application if not installed at the correct density; may be irritating to skin or upper respiratory tract; can hang up on wires, nails, or other obstructions in enclosed wall cavities; and needs relatively large application holes.

Fig. 9-4: Pouring vermiculite loose-fill insulation over fiberglass.

Rock Wool. Loose-fill rock and slag wool insulation has the following advantages and disadvantages:

Advantages. It has an R-value that is greater than loose fiberglass; has shorter fibers, so it can be blown through smaller holes; and is heavier and, therefore, does not hang up on obstructions in wall cavities as easily as fiberglass.

Disadvantages. It may settle after application if not applied at the correct density.

Cellulose Fiber. Cellulose fiber is manufactured from paper products, primarily recycled newsprint, or virgin wood fiber. The paper is shredded and milled to produce a fluffy, low-density material. Large amounts (up to 25% by weight) of chemicals, primarily boric acid, are added to provide flame resistance. Separation of these additives from the insulation materials has been reported, although there are no standard specifications to measure the permeance of these chemicals. The following are the advantages and disadvantages of cellulose fiber insulation:

Advantages.   It has a low cost/R-value, can be blown or poured into enclosed cavities, fills irregular horizontal spaces, and uses recycled newsprint.

Disadvantages.   It can absorb moisture, which may alter physical and chemical properties, and it may settle if not applied at correct density.

Perlite.   Perlite is a naturally occurring, siliceous, volcanic glass. Perlite ore is composed primarily of aluminum silicate. It is expanded to between 4 and 20 times its original volume to produce a pellet-like material that insulates with many tiny, glass-sealed air cells. It is usually poured into open cavities. The following are the advantages and disadvantages of perlite insulation:

Advantages.   It is easy to pour, fills irregular spaces; is rot, vermin, and termite resistant; and is noncorrosive and noncombustible. To increase its resistance to water absorption, nonflammable silicone is added.

Disadvantages.   It has an expensive, low R-value/inch; can absorb moisture if not treated; is heavy; and is not always compatible with other insulations.

Vermiculite.   Vermiculite is a mica-like, hydrated, laminar material. It consists of aluminum-iron-magnesium silicates with both free and bound water. When subjected to high temperatures, it expands and releases moisture. The advantages and disadvantages of vermiculite insulation are as follows:

Advantages.   It is similar to perlite.

Disadvantages.   It is similar to perlite, but with a lower R-value/inch.

Rigid Board

These materials are rigid or semirigid extrusions of cellular plastic. They are available in varying thicknesses, usually in 2' by 8' or 4' by 8' panels.

Extruded Polystyrene.   Polystyrene is a polymer material produced by an extrusion process that results in fine, closed cells containing a mixture of air and refrigerant gas (fluorocarbon). An aluminum sheet may be bonded to one or both surfaces. The advantages and disadvantages are as follows:

Advantages.   It has a high R-value, has excellent moisture resistance, has high structural strength (compared with other rigid board insulation), may serve as a vapor barrier, is easy to work with, can be used as sheathing, and is easy to install with adhesives (Fig. 9-5).

Fig. 9-5: Applying an adhesive to a rigid polystyrene board.

Disadvantages. It is expensive, is flammable (must be covered with a fire-protective covering), has refrigerant gas that may be harmful, must be protected from long-term direct exposure to ultraviolet light, and has degradation occurring at temperatures over 165°F.

Molded or Expanded Polystyrene. Molded or expanded polystyrene is also a styrene polymer produced by a mold/expansion process that results in coarse, closed cells containing air. It is often called *beadboard*. It has a lower R-value than extruded polystyrene, due both to its lower density and to the fact that its air cells do not contain refrigerant gas. The advantages and disadvantages are as follows:

Advantages. It is fairly moisture resistant, has a high R-value, is easy to work with, is the least expensive foam board insulation, can be used as sheathing, and is easy to install with adhesives.

Disadvantages. It must be protected from long-term exposure to ultraviolet light, is flammable (must be covered with a fire-protective covering), is more expensive than nonfoam insulations, and has degradation occurring over 165°F.

Polyurethane and Polyisocyanurate. These boards are plastic polymers formed by the same reaction processes as those which formed other foam boards but with slightly different chemicals. The result is an 80% to 90% closed-cell foam containing refrigerant gases instead of air. Aluminum foil skins are often placed on both surfaces. These combine with the high concentration of refrigerant gases to produce a very high R-value. The advantages and disadvantages are as follows:

Advantages. It has a high R-value, is easy to work with, is easy to install with adhesives, can be used as sheathing, and has high structural strength.

Disadvantages. It is very expensive; has dimensional shrinkage and expansion by temperature/moisture extremes; is flammable (must be covered by a fire-protective covering); and has an R-value that decreases as foam ages, especially when foam is not covered in foil.

Because of the flammability of *most* rigid board insulation materials, they should be stored and handled far from any potential fire hazards during installation.

Foamed-in-Place

One of the best insulating materials available today is polyurethane or polyiso-cyanate foam. One inch of polyurethane (often simply referred to as "urethane") has an R-value of 7.1. It is most commonly used in retrofitting metal and built-up flat roofs (Fig. 9-6). The foam is sprayed in place and covered by an elastomeric coating. Polyurethane foam is formed through the mixing of an "A" isocyanate component and a "B" resin component in a specially designed spray gun that dispenses the atomized, heated liquid mixture directly on the substrate. This liquid immediately expands to about thirty (30) times its volume and bonds tenaciously to the surface to which it is applied.

Layers or "lifts" of foam are sprayed in place to achieve the desired thickness of insulation. As these layers are sprayed, they bond and become homogeneous with previous layers. This sprayed-in-place insulation has no joints, seams, or

Fig. 9-6: Foamed-in-place insulation being applied.

cracks through which moisture, heat, or cold can enter. The foam flows into all cracks, around all protrusions, and into all cavities; it completely seals the surface.

To protect the polyurethane from moisture and sunlight, the insulation must be covered with an elastomeric coating. The coating is a synthetic, rubber-like fluid or liquid coating material that is sprayed or roller applied in multiple coats to achieve a prescribed thickness. It cures to form a flexible, weather-protective cover over the foam. Should any cracks or breaks develop in the foam surface, this rubber-like coating stretches to cover the crack and protect the surface.

Advantages. Polyurethane foam has a high R-value per inch. The spray application seals cracks and openings that would otherwise result in infiltration. The elastomeric coating makes the roof watertight.

Disadvantages. Such foamed-in-place roof systems are not normally considered for home installation. Roof systems should be applied by a professional. Because polyurethane foam is combustible and susceptible to ultraviolet deterioration, it must be protected.

Reflective

Aluminum foil, the major reflective surface insulation (Fig. 9-7), differs from other insulating materials in the manner in which it retards heat transfer. Unlike

Fig. 9-7: Reflective aluminum foil insulation being installed.

the others, foil operates by reflecting incident infrared radiation, thus reducing radiant heat transfer. Aluminum foil is the greatest benefit to those applications where conductive and convective heat losses are reduced already by conventional means.

Aluminum foil facings are sometimes used in conjunction with mineral fiber and rigid board foam insulations if an air space is adjacent to the foil. Multi-layered (accordion blankets) aluminum foil is sometimes used to insulate walls, floors, and windows. The advantages and disadvantages are as follows:

Advantages.   It has an excellent vapor barrier, is nonflammable, and takes up minimal space.

Disadvantages.   It requires air space between foil and wall surfaces, may constitute an electrical hazard if contact is made with live wires, has little effect on conduction or convection heat losses, is expensive, damages easily, has reduced effectiveness when reflective surface is dulled by water vapor or dust, needs to be used with other insulation to achieve overall high R-values, is not an air barrier unless the joints are taped, and is difficult to install effectively.

PURCHASE OF INSULATION

When you know how much and what kinds of insulation have already been installed in your home (see pages 26 and 27), it is possible to determine the amount needed to make your home fully energy efficient (see pages 25 and 27). As already discussed, the amount of insulation your home requires to be fully weatherized depends on the local climate, and on your microclimate—the placement of the house in relation to sunlight, wind, large trees, etc. Actually the amount of insulation you need also depends on both general factors and several *personal* factors, including the room temperature that you and your family find comfortable, the number of people who live in your house, how much time is spent and what activities are done in each area of your house, and how long you plan to live in it.

The general, nonpersonal factors determining the amount of insulation include your climate. Climate is always related to a given area, however; the size of the climatic reference area can vary enormously. When talking about the climate of large regions such as those shown in Fig. 3-2, we refer to it as a "macro-climate." Cities and portions of states are usually classified as having a "local climate." The smallest climatic area, such as a small town or even your home site, is called a "microclimate." It is because of the latter that winter can be colder around the corner than in your block.

Another general factor is the financial: When figuring the amount of insulation to install, keep in mind that there is a point of diminishing financial returns. That is, there comes a point when increasing the thickness of insulation does help save energy, but costs nearly as much to install as the small amount of additional energy it will save. In most areas of the Midwest, for instance, it will take about ten years to gain sufficient energy savings to equal the expense of adding ceiling insulation from R-11 to R-19. However, when you upgrade your insulation from nothing (about R-3 in most houses) to R-19, it will almost certainly pay you back in about five years.

It is very important, when purchasing insulation, to consider or include a vapor barrier to keep warm moist air from seeping into the insulation cavity of walls and ceilings and causing water condensation. Insulation that is allowed to absorb moisture loses its resistance to thermal transmission, since it is full of water, and water transmits heat a great deal easier than the dead air that normally fills the insulation (Fig. 9-8). Moisture also damages the wood framing by freezing and thawing in cycles and by encouraging the growth of fungus.

Vapor barriers should never be substituted for good ventilation. Proper ventilation will eliminate a good portion of the moisture that normally builds up in the area.

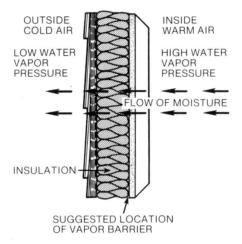

Fig. 9-8: Vapor flow through a house wall.

Insulating Attics and Ceilings **10**

It has been said that the first commandment of energy savings is "Insulate Thy Attic," and this rule can be applied with the greatest benefit in homes with uninsulated, unfinished attics. But some of these homes do not have a proper attic, and in some the attic space has been finished into additional living space. Adding insulation in these attics is not as simple as pouring cellulose between open joists or laying down fiberglass batts or blankets. Adding insulation to these areas will probably reduce your energy consumption, but the work and cost involved may outweigh the benefits. So consider all the factors involved before applying the first rule of energy savings to your home.

Figure 10-1 illustrates three types of housetop designs common to residential buildings. Each is insulated in a different manner. Regardless of your home's construction, it is extremely important that the structure be capped with a protective layer of insulation. In all homes, convective air currents transfer heat to the ceiling area where the heat is conducted away from the living area. Lack of a *thermal cap* to reduce this conduction will result in a serious loss of energy.

This chapter will explain how to insulate unfinished attics, completely finished attics, and cathedral ceilings. When capping your home with insulation, pay close attention to ventilation requirements. In every application, except *rooftop* insulation, water vapor and condensation must be controlled with the use of vapor barriers and ventilation.

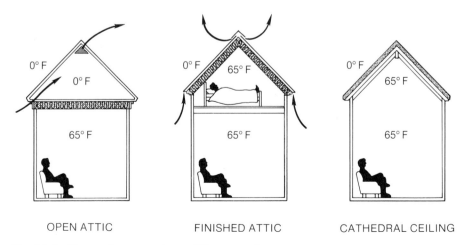

OPEN ATTIC   FINISHED ATTIC   CATHEDRAL CEILING

Fig. 10-1: Thermal caps on three different rooftops.

GENERAL PREPARATIONS AND PRECAUTIONS

Before climbing into the attic to begin the actual insulating job, first collect the tools and materials you will need to complete the job and to complete it safely.

If you are insulating an unfinished attic floor, you will require several solid planks to form a movable working platform (Fig. 10-2). An old door will also do this job nicely. Good footing is an important safety precaution. Losing your footing in an unfinished attic could cause serious personal injury and heavy damage to the ceiling below. So when working in an unfinished attic, do not, for any reason, step onto the ceiling below.

Fig. 10-2: Several boards make a platform from which to work safely.

Protruding roofing nails may also pose a safety hazard. Wear a hard hat or safety helmet to avoid a nasty cut. Provide enough light to allow you to see the work area. A mechanic's trouble light that can be hung where needed and moved from place to place is ideal.

When working with loose-fill insulation, have a rake or long board handy to level the insulation between the joists. If you are working with fiberglass or rock wool insulation, you will need a pair of gloves, an air filtering mask, and adequate clothing since fiberglass particles are very irritating if inhaled or if they work their way into your skin. Wear a long-sleeved shirt and long pants. Button your collar and cuffs, binding any loose cuffs with tape if need be. You will also need a heavy-duty stapler and a sharp knife or shears for cutting fiberglass or rock wool blankets to size. A roll of duct tape is also handy for taping any tears that may occur in the vapor barrier.

Repairing Roof Leaks and Electrical Wiring

Before installing the insulation, take some time to look for roof leaks and frayed electrical wiring. Wet insulation is ineffective in reducing heat, and will encourage fungus growth and decay. Wet spots, discoloration, and warped framing members indicate a leaking roof. Poke around with a screwdriver in suspicious-looking areas. If the wood is spongy and gives easily, you have a serious leakage problem. By all means, correct a leaky roof before insulating.

Do not lay insulation, especially cellulose, over faulty wiring. If your house is an older one, hire an inspector to check your wiring carefully. Replace defective wiring before insulating. You may wish to consider replacing recessed lighting fixtures with ones that are flush with the inside ceiling. This will eliminate another potential fire hazard as well as a serious heat leak.

Sealing the Attic Floor

Sealing openings in the attic floor is a preparative step often overlooked when insulating an attic (Fig. 10-3). Consequently, a lot of heat simply bypasses the insulation, and the efficiency of your attic is reduced to far less than the esti-mated R-value of the insulation. Heat rises into the attic through openings

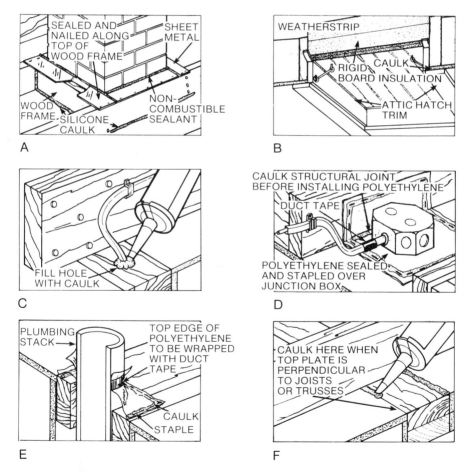

Fig. 10-3: To eliminate or reduce heat loss in the attic: (A) Seal around heating ducts, fan ducts, and the chimney; (B) seal the attic hatch; (C) around electrical cables; (D) junction boxes; (E) the plumbing stack; and (F) the tops of partition walls.

around flues, plumbing vents, electrical wires, recessed light fixtures, and chimneys. Chimneys are particularly notorious for heat leaks. In some houses framing members are built out several inches away from the chimney, which creates an escape hatch for heat all the way from the basement to the attic. The space between the frame and the chimney should be filled with unfaced fiberglass (most facings are combustible) or some other noncombustible material. Stuff the insulation in very tightly to prevent air drafts from blowing it aside. Provide an additional seal with duct tape or caulk. Do not overlook any other interior and exterior wall cavities. If these are not insulated, seal the openings with insulation.

INSULATING THE UNFINISHED ATTIC

With all the preliminary work completed, you can begin insulating the attic. Keep in mind that the insulation should always envelop the warm-in-winter living areas and separate them from unheated areas. It would be inefficient to place insulation in the rafters of an unfinished, unheated attic. Heat from the room below would simply escape through the gable and soffit vents. Therefore, always place the insulation in the floor of an unheated, unfinished attic.

The first step is to provide a vapor barrier between the insulation and the warm-in-winter room below. You can purchase batts or blankets with vapor barriers already attached to the insulation (Fig. 10-4), but a sheet of polyethylene provides a much more efficient vapor barrier. Lay the plastic on the floor between the joists and staple the plastic to the sides of the joists. Staple the edges flat against the joists. Do not leave any puckers or fish mouths that will permit water vapor to escape into the insulation. Overlap the ends of each sheet at least 6" and tape with duct tape.

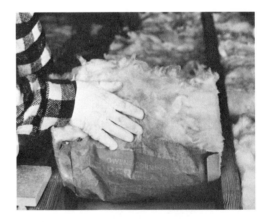

Fig. 10-4: Fiberglass batt with attached vapor barrier.

Insulating with Batts or Blankets

Either batt, blanket, or loose-fill insulation may now be placed between the joists and on top of the polyethylene. If insulating with batts or blankets, the insulation should completely fill the space between floor joists. Any gaps will allow heat to bypass the insulation and escape. If irregular spacing results in voids, either cut strips to fill the void or stuff the space with leftover pieces of insulation. Batts and blankets are easy to cut. Simply lay a board on top of the insulation to use as a straightedge. Kneel on the board, and with a sharp knife, slice through the insulation. When laying the insulation, start from the eaves and work your way toward the center of the attic. The insulation should completely cover the attic floor including the exterior wall cavities, but should not block the soffit vents. If necessary, make baffles and place them at the ends of each joist (Fig. 10-5) to prevent the insulation from blocking the flow of air between soffit vents and ridge or gable vents.

Cross bracing presents a minor problem when insulating with batt or blanket. Uninsulated cross bracing will result in heat leaks. The solution is simple. Slice a batt down the middle for a distance of about 12″ and slip the two resulting tongues over and under the cross bracing (Fig. 10-6). Follow the same procedure for both sides of the bracing. If you are using loose-fill insulation, simply pack the bracing with insulation.

Fig. 10-5: When insulating an attic, install baffles to prevent blocking soffit vents.

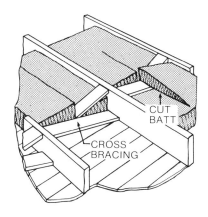

Fig. 10-6: Installing insulation at cross bracing.

The National Electric Code requires you to keep insulation at least 3" away from recessed light fixtures (Fig. 10-7). The waste heat from the lights over a prolonged period will char and possibly ignite combustible materials (such as vapor barriers).

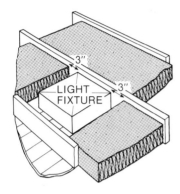

Fig. 10-7: Keep insulation 3" away from recessed light fixtures.

Adding Insulation

If you already have insulation in your attic but wish to add more, either batt, loose-fill, or a combination of both can be used. If you choose to use batts, lay the batts perpendicular to the joists so that the joists are completely covered with insulation (Fig. 10-8). This will eliminate the joists as weak spots in your attic insulation. **CAUTION:** Never place a vapor barrier on top of existing insulation. The barrier will trap moisture in the insulation beneath and ruin its effectiveness. If you must use faced insulation, slash the facing into ribbons so that water vapor may escape (Fig. 10-9). Be careful to maintain the 3" spacing between insulation and recessed light fixtures, and avoid blocking the air pathways under the eave rafters.

Fig. 10-8: Lay added insulation across floor joists.

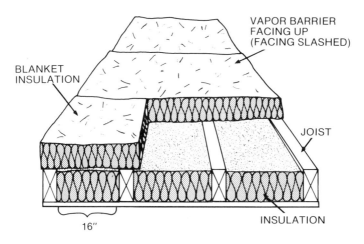

Fig. 10-9: Slash vapor barrier with knife when adding insulation to existing insulation.

INSULATING A FINISHED ATTIC

Insulating a finished attic requires a great deal of planning and work. Since the attic is heated, the insulation must be placed not in the floor but in the end walls, knee walls, rafters, and collar beams (Fig. 10-10). And if the finished area does not fill the entire attic, insulation must also be placed in the floor of the unfinished, unheated areas. Getting to these areas can be a problem. If you desire to remodel the interior, you can simply install rigid board insulation if loose-fill or batts and blankets cannot be installed without a lot of difficulty on the interior wall surfaces. Always consider the expense, labor time, and other factors involved before choosing the best way to insulate your finished attic.

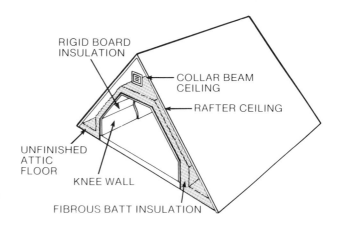

Fig. 10-10: An insulated finished attic.

Insulating Knee Walls

Begin by providing a vapor barrier between the attic room and the insulation. The best way to do this is to staple polyethylene plastic between the knee wall studs. Cut strips of plastic 2" longer and 2" wider than the cavity between the two studs, and staple the strips to the sides of the studs and to the lower sills. Batts with a vapor barrier facing may also be used in this situation, but because the vapor barrier must face the warm-in-winter living space, it cannot be stapled to the studs; therefore, moisture will seep around the edges of the facing, bypassing the vapor barrier and infiltrating the insulation.

After you have the polyethylene stapled in position, place unfaced batts between the studs (Fig. 10-11). The batts should be slightly wider than the width of the cavity in order to provide a friction fit. Fill the cavity from side to side and from the sill to the top of the studs. Do not extend the insulation all the way up to the roof decking between the rafters. An air space must remain between the insulation and the decking to permit ventilation. If the insulation does not fit snugly between the studs, the batts can be held in place with wire or nylon string laced back and forth between nails driven into the faces of the studs. Batts with attached vapor barriers may also be attached to the back side of the interior wall with a spray adhesive.

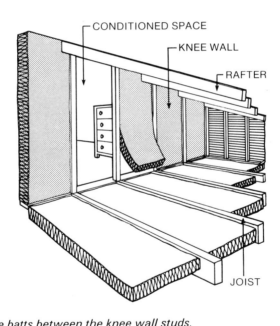

Fig. 10-11: Place batts between the knee wall studs.

The studs in a knee wall are usually 2 by 4s, and the amount of insulation that can be placed between them is limited. With the use of *spindle anchors,* additional insulation can be added. As shown in Fig. 10-12, unfaced blanket insulation can be impaled on the spindles that are bonded to the studs. Following the manufacturer's directions, apply adhesive to the base of the spindle and press the spindle to the stud (Fig. 10-12A). Space the spindles 8" apart so that each length of insulation is secured to two spindles on each stud. Install the blanket insulation horizontally so that the complete wall area including the studs can be covered. Begin at the bottom and work up. Press the blanket on the spindles and secure with the self-locking washers (Fig. 10-12B). Press each additional blanket tightly against the one below it. Trim the top blanket so that it does not inhibit ventilation between the roof rafters.

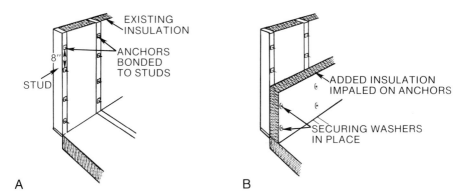

Fig. 10-12: To add extra insulation to knee walls: (A) Bond spindle anchors to 2 by 4; and (B) press insulation over spindle and secure with self-locking washers.

Insulating the Rafters

The sloped ceiling beneath the rafters is a trouble spot. The cavities between the rafters are practically inaccessible, and the cavities must be kept partially open so that air can circulate under the roof sheathing. Loose-fill insulation is not applicable in this situation; it would simply spill out of the lower opening. A batt or blanket could possibly be pushed up the lengths of the cavities with a long pole, but protruding roofing nails often make this impossible. Even if you do successfully slip insulation between the rafters, the batt or blanket must not be so thick that it cuts off ventilation from the soffit vents to the ridge vent. An air space of at least 1″ must be maintained between the insulation and the roof sheathing (Fig. 10-13).

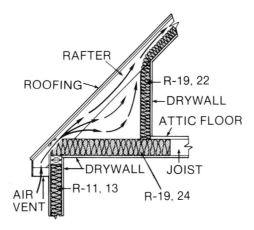

Fig. 10-13: Maintain a 1″ air space above the rafter insulation to allow air circulation.

Insulating the Collar Beams

The flat portion of an attic ceiling is suspended below collar beams. If access into this area is not already provided by a hatch of some sort, cut an accessway through the ceiling following the same procedures for cutting an accessway through a knee wall. Cut the hole to a size that is just large enough for you to enter.

Once you gain access into the collar beam area, insulate the ceiling as you would an attic floor. Staple polyethylene plastic between the collar beams to serve as a vapor barrier. Make sure that the edges of the plastic are stapled against the sides of the beams. Any gaps in the plastic will allow water vapor to seep into the insulation.

Then, either lay unfaced batts or pour loose-fill into the cavities between the collar beams. Install baffles between the collar beams where the collar beams meet the rafters; this will prevent the insulation from blocking the air circulation from soffit vent to ridge vent, and will prevent the loose-fill insulation from falling down between the rafters.

Insulating the End Walls

In a finished attic, the end walls are inaccessible. It is impossible to install batts or blankets in these areas without tearing out the finished walls. The only alternative is to blow loose-fill insulation into the wall cavities. You can hire a contractor to blow loose-fill into the spaces, or if you are extremely enterprising, and have two or three helpful friends to assist you, you can rent blowing equipment and do the job yourself. Review the manufacturer's instructions, and any directions the rental agency can provide, before using the machine.

INSULATING A FINISHED ATTIC WITH RIGID BOARD INSULATION

The problems and shortcomings of insulating a finished attic with blankets or loose-fill can be overcome by insulating with rigid board insulation. If you intend to remodel the attic anyway, placing rigid board insulation on the interior wall surfaces should be considered seriously. Rigid board insulation can be used alone, or it can be used in addition to blanket and loose-fill insulation to increase the R-value of the total insulation. Another advantage of installing rigid board insulation over the interior walls is that accessways and blowing holes cut into the old wall and ceiling panels do not have to be resealed. The insulation and new wall finish (usually gypsum drywall) will hide these openings. Before you begin, have an electrician install light fixtures, switches, and electrical outlets flush with the new surfaces.

Installing Insulation

Begin with the ceiling. Use polystyrene or urethane rigid boards that are at least 2″ thick. These are available in sheets measuring 4 by 8 or 2 by 8.

Cut the boards to fit by scoring the boards with a utility knife or razor blade and snapping the boards along the line. Nail the insulation through the ceiling material and into the rafters or collar beams. Use large-head, galvanized nails, such as roofing nails. Space the nails 8″ on center and penetrate the wood at least 1-1/4″.

Applying insulation to the knee walls and end walls does not require any nailing. Cut the insulation to fit and bond it directly to the old wall surfaces. Apply the adhesives in 1/4″ ribbons spaced 16″ apart. Extrude a ribbon of adhesive around the perimeter of each board 1″ in from the centers. (Remember that many adhesives react chemically with plastic foams. Only use adhesives specifically formulated for bonding rigid board insulations.) Do one board at a time and press each one firmly to the substrate to ensure a solid bond. Let the adhesive cure for 24 hours before installing drywall.

Installing Drywall Over Rigid Board

The 4′ wide by 8′ high gypsum sheets are usually applied to walls vertically, but can be installed horizontally on the walls after the ceiling has been covered (Fig. 10-14). The horizontal method of application is ideal if your knee walls are 4′

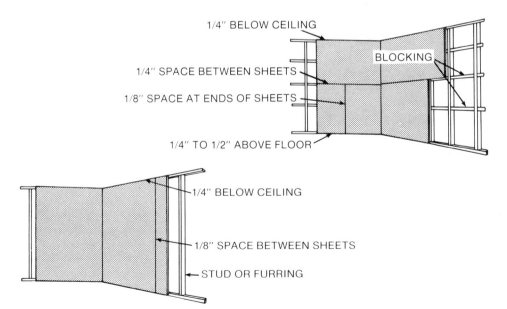

Fig. 10-14: Gypsum drywall can be installed either vertically or horizontally over any smooth structurally sound surface, on furring strips, or directly onto studs.

high, because it minimizes the number of vertical joints. Also, plan to work from the top of the room down, i.e., the ceiling and/or top half of the walls, in that order. On walls, this approach provides a better joint, and panels already installed are less likely to be marred by other panels being handled. Where joints are necessary, they should be made at windows or doors. End joints over openings should be on studs.

When installing predecorated or finished gypsum boards, the use of panel adhesive is almost a "must."

When using an adhesive, however, the panels should be preconditioned by a simple "bowing" procedure. This assures pressure at the center for maximum contact while the adhesive sets. To accomplish this panel bow, cut the panels (cutting details are given later in the chapter) to the proper ceiling height (1/4" to 1/2" shorter than floor-to-ceiling height, to compensate for uneven ceilings and avoid having to force panels into position). Then, stack the panels as shown in Fig. 10-15, using 4" high wood blocks to create the "bow." Two 2 by 4s running across the width of the stack are ideal. Stack with the finished face down. Pad the wood block with carpeting or similar material to prevent damage to the finished surface. Proper bowing can take from one to several days, depending on humidity conditions.

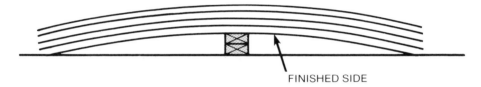

FINISHED SIDE

Fig. 10-15: Method of bowing drywall.

Ceiling drywall is attached first. Install the panels at right angles to the rafters and collar beams. Apply 1/4" beads of adhesive to the back side of the drywall in vertical strips, 12" to 16" apart and 3/4" to 1" in from each edge. Place the panel into position. Holding the ceiling board in position can be difficult. If you are working alone, you can solve this problem by making a "T" brace of a 2' long 1 by 4 nailed to the end of a 2 by 4 of sufficient length to reach from the floor to the height of the ceiling. The T-brace can be used to hold the panel until the adhesive sets. Nails should also be used to support a panel while the adhesive dries. On ceiling installations, nailing should be spaced 6" to 8" around the perimeter of the drywall. The nails should be long enough to penetrate 1-1/4" into the wood. Two or three nails should be used in the center (field) of the board. These center nails can either be removed or driven through the gypsum board, and the holes can be spackled after 24 hours.

Install drywall over the wall insulation with adhesive and a minimum of nails. Apply adhesive to the back side of the drywall as described in the previous paragraph. With a board scrap, block the bottom of the panel up to 1/4" to 1/2" from the floor. Press the panel firmly to the wall using a sliding motion to spread the adhesive. Nail at the top. Remove the block and nail across the bottom. With your room completely walled, you can now finish the installation by taping and cementing joints, filling hammerhead dimples, and smoothing over any possible surface irregularities.

OTHER DRYWALL INSTALLATIONS

Gypsum drywall paneling is also employed in many home remodeling projects. When installing this paneling in a room with rough plaster walls or masonry walls, furring strips must first be attached to the wall. The vertical furring strip that will support the starting edge of the starting panel is butted snugly against the adjoining wall. The first panel is also butted against the adjoining wall. The width of this panel determines the location of the centerline of the second vertical furring strip. Each following vertical strip should be spaced so that the panel edges cover one half of each strip. The centers of each horizontal strip should be spaced 16" apart, with a strip framing each door and window. When panels are applied to masonry walls below grade, the use of a vapor barrier, such as plastic, foil, or a sealant, between the wall and the paneling is recommended.

This same system of furring strip installation is also used when paneling over very uneven walls or walls with a rough-textured surface. In order to make a level surface or plumb wall, place small shims under the furring strips wherever needed. The furring strips should be entirely free of dust, oil, and other dirt and contaminants. Remember, for proper bonding of any adhesive the surfaces to be bonded must always be clean.

Gypsum panels may also be applied directly to the studding. Recommended stud spacing is 16" on centers. Studs where panel edges are to be bonded receive two continuous 1/4" beads of adhesive, one near each edge of the stud face. Intermediate studs receive *one* continuous 1/4" bead of adhesive approximately centered on the stud face. After pressing the panel into position, nail the panel along the top and bottom ends. These nails will later be covered by the base and cove molding. The bottom of the panel should be about 1/4" off the floor. With uniform hand pressure, press the panel into full contact with the adhesive bead. Adjacent panels should make only moderate contact and never be forced together.

INSULATING CATHEDRAL CEILINGS

The rustic grandeur created by the sloping heights and exposed beams of cathedral ceilings makes them a popular choice of both architects and home-owners. Yet cathedral ceilings waste heat energy. A typical cathedral ceiling may offer just 2" of pine board, a layer of roofing felt, and shingles as a barrier against the winter cold. The resistance value of such a roof is approximately R-2.7.

If you feel it is time to sacrifice aesthetics for economy, then insulating a cathedral ceiling is a simple operation. But if you want to spare your maple decking and magnificent exposed beams, then insulating a cathedral ceiling will involve plenty of work and expense.

Insulating with Batts or Blankets

If you are willing to cover the exposed beams, a cathedral ceiling can be insulated with batt or blanket insulation and then covered with drywall or tongue-and-groove planking (Fig. 10-16). To do so, beams must be spaced 16" or 24" apart. Use faced insulation of a thickness that will allow a 1" to 2" space between the insulation and the roof for air circulation. Install eave vents and ridge vents if necessary to provide sufficient ventilation.

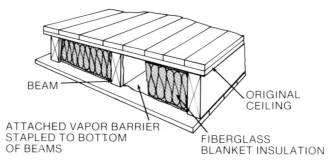

BEAM

ATTACHED VAPOR BARRIER
STAPLED TO BOTTOM
OF BEAMS

ORIGINAL
CEILING

FIBERGLASS
BLANKET INSULATION

Fig. 10-16: Insulating a cathedral ceiling with fiberglass batt insulation.

Staple the flange of the vapor barrier to the face of the beams. Be careful not to leave any puckers or gaps in the flange that will permit moisture to invade the insulation. When stapling is complete, cover the entire ceiling with gypsum drywall or tongue-and-groove boards. Because of the height involved, consider having a contractor do the finishing work.

If you feel confident that you can do the finishing work yourself, secure a set of sturdy scaffolding and enlist several helpers. Plan your work so that the drywall panels lay across the beams. Cut the panels so that the edges fall on the center of the beams.

Extrude a 1/4" serpentine strip of gypsum drywall adhesive to the beams. Only extrude enough adhesive to install one panel at a time. Nail the panels with broadhead drywall nails that will penetrate at least 1-1/4" into the beam. Space the nails 8" apart. Spackle and paint.

Installing Insulation between the Beams

One way to preserve rustic beams is to place 2" vinyl-faced pressed fiberglass panels between the beams. The panels are available in several textured vinyl faces and are fastened on the underside of the roof with quarter-round molding (Fig. 10-17). The 2" panels have an R-value of 9, are lightweight and easy to handle, and are available in sizes up to 4' by 16'.

A spray adhesive (a synthetic elastomer) simplifies installation. First, use a utility knife to cut the panels to fit between the beams. Spray the adhesive to the decking between the beams and press the first panel into place. Hold it in place until the adhesive grabs. The adhesive will hold the panel in place while you secure it with quarter-round molding. Nail the molding around the perimeter of the panel. Never use adhesive without nailing.

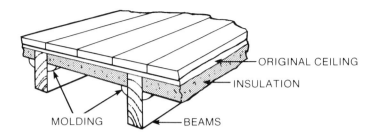

Fig. 10-17: Vinyl-faced fiberglass attached with quarter-round molding.

You may also place rigid board insulation between the beams. Select the type that will give you the highest possible R-value while sacrificing the least amount of exposed beam.

With 1" urethane tongue-and-groove boards you can achieve an R-value of 7 or more while sacrificing less of the beams. These can be purchased with foil backing and foil facing to provide additional fireproofing for your ceiling. Because urethane is flammable, you should also cover the boards with gypsum drywall.

First, be sure that the surface to which you will be bonding the insulation is structurally sound, clean, dry, and flat. It must be free of grease, loose paint, and wallpaper. Remove any ceiling molding and caulk any cracks where the ceiling and walls meet (Fig. 10-18A). Apply a panel and foam adhesive to the insulation boards in 1/4" ribbons spaced 16" apart or in golf-ball-sized ribbons spaced 12". Press firmly over every square foot of insulation to ensure a firm bond. The adhesive will hold the insulation temporarily until you install the drywall. Apply panel and foam adhesive in ribbons to the 1/2" drywall according to instructions on the adhesive cartridge. Install the drywall against the foam. Press firmly and uniformly across every square foot of surface to assure a permanent bond. While holding drywall in the final position, nail with pairs of nails on 16" centers in both directions. Nails should penetrate into roof deck at least 1-1/4". They must not penetrate through the roof deck. Nails must be used on ceiling applications due to the weight of the gypsum wallboard.

Spackle, tape, and sand the drywall joints. Where the drywall butts into the exposed rafters or beams, install quarter-round molding to cover the joints (Fig. 10-18B).

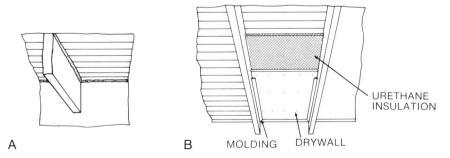

Fig. 10-18: When insulating with urethane and drywall, (A) seal the edges with caulk and (B) apply urethane and drywall with adhesive and nails.

ATTIC VENTILATION

There are two basic climatic conditions that exist in every attic; summer heat and winter moisture. Ventilation offers the most effective means of preventing or correcting the problems caused by these two conditions.

There are five basic types of attic ventilators: ridge, roof, undereave, triangular gable end, and rectangular gable end (Fig. 10-19). These will do a satisfactory job with most roof designs. Also they will blend with any style of architecture.

To tell exactly how much ventilation is needed for your home, it is necessary to determine the area (in square feet) of your attic floor, and relate that to the *free area* of the ventilation system you have selected. Free area is the approximate area of the clear or free opening of the ventilator, through which air can actually move.

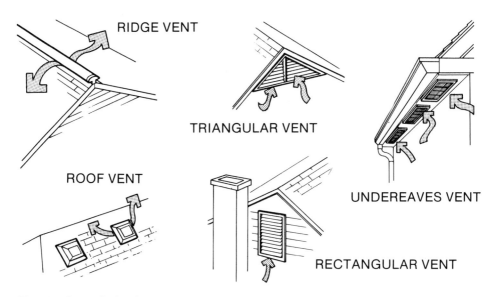

RIDGE VENT

TRIANGULAR VENT

ROOF VENT

UNDEREAVES VENT

RECTANGULAR VENT

Fig. 10-19: Typical attic vents.

The ratio of free area to the area to be ventilated should be about 1/150. This means that for each 150 square feet of attic floor space, 1 square foot of free area is required. If at least 50% of the required ventilating area is provided by ventilators located in the upper portion of the space to be ventilated (at least 3 feet above the undereaves vents) and the remainder of the required ventilation provided by undereaves vents, the ratio can be reduced to 1/300, or 1 square foot of free area to every 300 square feet of attic space. Attic space should also include porch roofs, canopies, and any other connected structures where condensation may occur. All spaces should be cross ventilated.

Ventilator openings should be screened and protected from the entrance of rain and snow. If undereaves vents are not used, the above total free area requirement must be doubled. This is equivalent to 1/150 ratio. Even if your attic area is presently vented, it should be carefully checked to determine whether or not the present vent arrangement is adequate to provide proper ventilation.

Insulating Walls 11

After putting a thermal cap on your house, the next place to protect against heat loss is the walls. Walls usually present the greatest surface area for conducted heat loss—two to four times as much area as the attic. Unfortunately, insulating a finished wall is not as simple as pouring cellulose in an unfinished attic floor. Depending on several factors, which we will discuss in this chapter, the insulation may be best placed in the wall, on the interior wall surface, or on the exterior wall surface. You may have to blow it in, staple it to, nail it on, or glue it to the walls. Before you are done, you may choose to build a wall frame, repanel your walls, or install new siding.

Insulating a wall can be a major undertaking, but the use of construction adhesives will simplify the difficult as well as the easy applications. By wrapping your walls in a cozy thermal blanket, you will expend less energy in order to keep your house a comfortable place in which to live—and that is what insulating is all about.

INSTALLING BATT OR BLANKET INSULATION— NEW CONSTRUCTION

Insulating walls with fiberglass or rock wool batt or blanket insulation is only possible when the wall cavities are exposed. That is why you should never miss a chance to add batt or blanket insulation during the construction of new walls or room additions.

Wall studs are commonly spaced 16″ or 24″ on center, and batt and blanket insulation is designed to fit snugly between them. The width of the strips is sufficient to create a friction fit between the insulation and the studs so no additional fasteners are necessary.

A vapor barrier should always be placed between the wall insulation and the warm-in-winter living space. Batts and blankets are available with two types of attached vapor barrier facings—those of kraft paper and those of foil. Kraft paper facings should be stapled to the face of the stud (Fig. 11-1A), but foil facings should be stapled to the inside edge of the stud (Fig. 11-1B). Stapling the foil to the inside edge of the stud (referred to as *inset* stapling) provides a dead air space that aids the foil in reflecting heat and adds to the R-value of the insulation. Do not leave any gaps along the flange edge; staple the facing tightly to the stud so that water vapor will not seep past the vapor barrier.

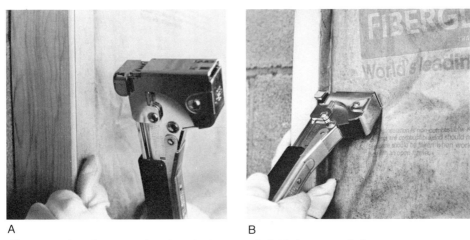

A   B

Fig. 11-1: Stapling vapor barrier: (A) face stapled; (B) inset stapled.

Completely fill the wall cavity with insulation. If using 8' batts, make sure that no gaps are left around the sill plate (Fig. 11-2A). Stuff insulation into voids, especially around window frames and doorframes (Fig. 11-2B). If blankets are used instead of batts, cut the blankets slightly longer than necessary to fill the space so that the facing may be peeled back and stapled to the top and bottom sills.

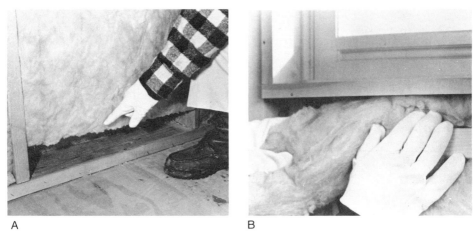

A   B

Fig. 11-2: Do not leave voids in the wall cavities.

Finishing the Walls

Once the installation of batt or blanket insulation is complete, the walls must be finished. One of the easiest and most popular finishing methods is the installation of plywood paneling using a paneling adhesive.

Plywood panels come in woods ranging from richly figured oak, mahogany, birch, and walnut to fir and pine, allowing a choice of decorative material to meet every taste and budget. They can be applied effectively to either traditional or modern interiors.

One outstanding advantage of plywood for interiors is the elimination of periodic redecorating and patching of cracks. Plywood walls are kickproof, punctureproof, and crackproof. The only upkeep required is an occasional waxing. The large sheets, 4' wide, 8' long, and 1/4" thick, can be erected quickly and easily with ordinary hand tools.

Estimating the Amount of Plywood Required. To estimate the number of panels required, measure the perimeter of the room. This is merely the total of the widths of each wall in the room. Use conversion Table 11-1 to figure the number of panels needed.

Table 11-1: Panel Estimation	
Perimeter (feet)	Number of 4' by 8' Panels Needed
36	9
40	10
44	11
48	12
52	13
56	14
60	15
64	16
68	17
72	18
92	23

For example, if your room walls measured 14' + 14' + 16' + 16', this would equal 60' or 15 panels required. To allow for areas such as windows, doors, fireplaces, etc., use the following deductions:

Door	1/2 panel
Window	1/4 panel
Fireplace	1/2 panel

If a room of this perimeter (60') had two windows, two doors, and a fireplace, the actual number of panels needed would be 13 (15 panels minus two total deductions). If the perimeter of the room falls between the figures in Table 11-1, use the next highest number to determine panels required. These figures are for rooms with 8' ceiling heights or less. For walls over 8' high, select a paneling that has V-grooves and that will stack, allowing panel grooves to line up perfectly from floor to ceiling.

Installing Plywood Paneling. After purchasing the necessary paneling, store the panels in the room for a few days before you start the job. Spacers allow air to circulate around each panel. For studs spaced 16" on center, use 1/4" plywood; for studs placed 24" or more on center, apply 3/4" furring strips.

Plan the sequence of panels about the room so that the natural color variations form a pleasing pattern in complementary tones or in direct contrast. Hold each panel against the wall to see how it looks before you nail it.

There are several tricks for laying out panels to reduce cutting as well as to achieve a pleasing pattern of joints. To avoid intricate fitting around windows and doors, start full panels on each side of the openings. On plain walls, it is best to start at the center so that fractional panels will be the same at each end. You can keep all joints vertical, the simplest arrangement, or use the tops and bottoms of windows as guidelines for horizontal joints.

To bond the paneling to the studs, extrude a panel adhesive in continuous or intermittent beads onto each stud (Fig. 11-3). Once the adhesive is applied, the panel may be pressed against the wall. It may be moved as much as is required for satisfactory adjustment. To make this easier, drive three or four small finishing nails about halfway in through the panel near the top edge. The panel can then be pulled away from the wall at the bottom with the nails acting as a hinge. After adjustment has been made, a padded block should be used to keep the panel pressed back on the wall, and then the nails are driven home. (These will be covered by a molding.) A rubber mallet or a hammer and padded block should be used on the face of the panel to assure good adhesive contact between panel and wall.

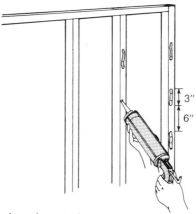

Fig. 11-3: Apply glue intermittently to studs.

Be sure that the panels are square with the adjacent wall (at corners) and ceiling before nailing. If the panel is not square with the adjacent wall, scribe it to the corner (Fig. 11-4). Keep the bottom of each wall panel about 1/4" above the floor to allow space for the lever used to pry the panel tightly against the ceiling. As the panels go up, keep checking them for plumbness. Shim out the studs or fill hollows of the framing. Keep a level handy for truing up and down (vertical position). Molding will take care of the irregular meeting with floor and ceiling. When nailing, start along one edge of the panel and work across the width so as to avoid bulges.

To locate an electrical outlet cutout on a panel, place the panel against the wall and, with a padded block over the approximate location of the outlet, tap it soundly with a hammer. The outlet box will indent the back side of the panel. Drill small pilot holes from the back (enlarge holes from finish side) and saw the outlet hole from the front side of the panel with a keyhole saw (Fig. 11-5). After the cutout has been made and the panel board installed, attach receptacle exten-

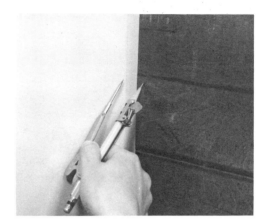

Fig. 11-4: A panel edge can be cut to fit an out-of-square corner by tracing the corner with a scriber.

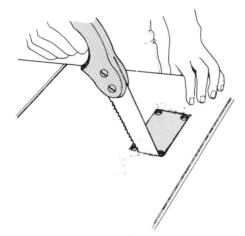

Fig. 11-5: Cut outlet box opening by drilling and sawing with a keyhole saw.

sions to advance the receptacles flush with the panel surface. Building codes usually require the front of the receptacle to be placed within 1/8" of the panel face. You should check the building codes for your specific locality.

INSULATING INTERIOR WALLS WITH RIGID BOARD INSULATION

Another way of insulating the walls of your home is to bond rigid board polystyrene insulation directly to the interior wall surfaces. There is no need to expose the wall cavities, and the use of the proper panel and foam adhesive makes the job fast and simple. In addition, you need not insulate your entire home at once to achieve good results. Insulating just one room—the one in which the family spends the most time—is a great way to produce a warm and comfortable living space.

Because rigid board polystyrene insulation burns easily, it must always be covered with a 15-minute fire-rated material such as 1/2" drywall or fire-rated wood paneling. These finishing materials can also be applied with adhesive and/or nails.

To begin the installation of the rigid board insulation, be sure the surface to which you will be bonding is structurally sound, clean, and dry. It must be free of grease, loose paint, and wallpaper. Remove baseboards, moldings, and window and door trim from all walls to be insulated. The surface of your new wall will probably extend out beyond your existing window frames and doorframes. If you are not qualified to do this work, hire a contractor or handyman to extend the frames and electrical boxes. If drywall will be used as the finishing material, nail wood nailers along the top and bottom edges of the wall (Fig. 11-6A).

Now that you have the room readied for insulation, cut the insulation to fit around any surface projections such as windows, nailers, electrical outlets, and conduits. This is accomplished easily with any sharp knife by scoring and snapping the rigid boards. You can also cut all the way through the insulation with a circular saw.

Next, apply a panel and foam adhesive in globs about the size of golf balls all around the perimeter and across the face of the first board. Space the globs 12" apart. Do one board of insulation at a time. When adhesive has been applied, place the insulation (horizontally or vertically) against the old wall surface. Press the insulation uniformly against the wall, applying pressure over every square foot to assure a permanent bond. Repeat this action for every board of insulation.

Where stud cavities contain water or drain pipes, cut away the existing plaster or wallboard over these cavities. Place fibrous insulation between the pipes and the outside wall (Fig. 11-6B). This will help prevent frozen pipes during the winter months. Next, replace the wallboard or plaster you have removed with wood nailer strips that match the thickness of the plaster and the rigid board insulation. Fasten several of these strips over the cavity. Be sure to leave some air space between the strips for heat to get through to the pipes. Do not cover

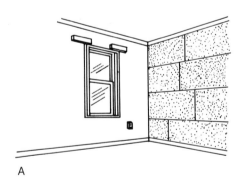

A

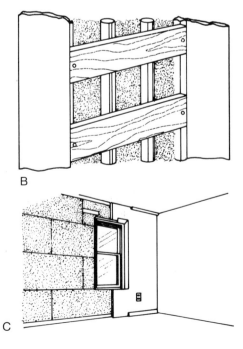

B

Fig. 11-6: To insulate an interior wall with rigid board: (A) Install nailers and place insulation between nailers; (B) place insulation behind pipes to prevent them from freezing; (C) install drywall over nailers and insulation.

C

these cavities with insulation. Nail your new wallboard directly to the cavity nailer strips.

When all the surfaces to be insulated have been covered with rigid board insulation, it is possible to finish the job by applying drywall or wood paneling over the rigid board (Fig. 11-6C). The finishing material should be cut to fit the entire height of the wall. Cut out any openings for electrical outlets and switches as needed. Allow the rigid board insulation to set for 24 hours before applying the finishing material. Apply panel and foam adhesive to the back of the drywall or wood paneling in the same manner as you did the insulation. Bond paneling directly to insulation with proper adhesive. Make sure the adhesive is compatible with the foam. Apply pressure over every square foot of surface. If using drywall as a finishing material, fasten the drywall to the wood nailers with drywall nails on 6" centers.

INSULATING MASONRY WALLS

Masonry walls are commonplace in homes today. Basement and crawl space walls are usually made of concrete blocks or poured concrete. Many wood frame homes are also partially or completely veneered with brick. Masonry frame homes, as opposed to wood frame homes, are also increasing in popularity as research reveals their superior rain penetration resistance, excellent thermal capabilities, and high fire resistance. There are a variety of ways to insulate a masonry wall, many of which are discussed in the following paragraphs.

Insulating the exterior surface of masonry walls has several benefits. Insulation placed on the exterior reduces *thermal shock* to the load-bearing wall, thus increasing its life by decreasing deterioration. Thermal short circuits are more easily avoided or eliminated and air infiltration is reduced. In addition, in masonry and concrete structures thermal mass is enclosed by the insulation membrane, which permits more efficient storage of heat.

Insulating Masonry Walls—Exterior

One simple, attractive, and effective method is illustrated in Fig. 11-7. In this method, exterior basement walls are insulated with urethane rigid board insulation that the manufacturer prebonds to a nail base. The insulation is glued and nailed in place. Decorative batten strips cover the nailheads to enhance aesthetic appearance.

The first step in this installation is to install a drip cap at the top of the wall (Fig. 11-8A). The drip cap must be wide enough to shield the insulation and siding.

Remove any dirt and dust from the block surface. Apply a panel and foam adhesive to the back of the insulation panel as shown in Fig. 11-8B. The bead should be 3/16" in diameter. Place the top edge of the corner panel against the drip cap (Fig. 11-8C), and apply pressure all over the panel to ensure complete contact of the adhesive with the masonry surface.

Mark the locations of batten strips on the panel surface. Using these marks as a guide, attach the panel to the block wall with masonry nails or power nails. Be

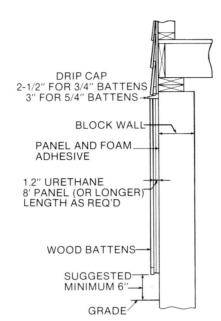

DRIP CAP
2-1/2″ FOR 3/4″ BATTENS
3″ FOR 5/4″ BATTENS

BLOCK WALL

PANEL AND FOAM
ADHESIVE

1.2″ URETHANE
8′ PANEL (OR LONGER)
LENGTH AS REQ'D

WOOD BATTENS

SUGGESTED
MINIMUM 6″

GRADE

Fig. 11-7: Detail of exterior masonry wall insulated with combination nail base and urethane.

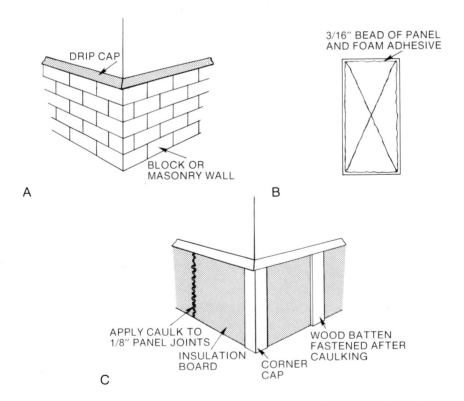

DRIP CAP

BLOCK OR
MASONRY WALL

A

3/16″ BEAD OF PANEL
AND FOAM ADHESIVE

B

APPLY CAULK TO
1/8″ PANEL JOINTS

INSULATION
BOARD

CORNER
CAP

WOOD BATTEN
FASTENED AFTER
CAULKING

C

Fig. 11-8: To insulate an exterior masonry wall: (A) Install drip cap; (B) apply adhesive to back of panel; and (C) place panel in position.

sure that the area in which all nails are driven will be covered by the batten strips.

Proceed in this manner until all the panels have been installed. Allow a 1/8" gap between the panels at all joints, and fill the joints with an acrylic latex caulk. Paint the batten strips with a primer and nail them in place using 2" ring-shank, corrosion-resistant nails. Apply a priming coat to the entire wall. If unevenness in the wall creates voids behind the batten strips, fill these voids with an acrylic latex caulk after priming and apply a finishing coat of paint.

Exterior masonry walls can also be finished with stucco installed over a layer of rigid board insulation (Fig. 11-9). Begin this job by cleaning all oil, grease, and dirt from the masonry wall. Once the wall is completely clean, attach furring strips of the same thickness as the rigid board insulation to the wall. Space furring strips 2' apart so that a 2' wide piece of rigid board insulation can fit between them. Nail the furring strips in place with masonry nails or anchors.

Bond the insulation to the masonry wall with a panel and foam adhesive. Follow the manufacturer's directions concerning application of the adhesive. The insulation should fit snugly between the strips. To finish the job, fasten expanded metal lath to the furring strips and apply a conventional three-coat stucco finish. Follow the specific installation instructions of the stucco manufacturer.

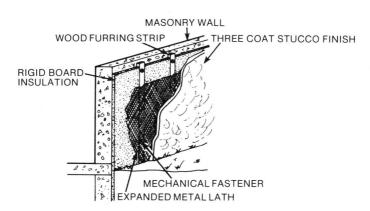

Fig. 11-9: Insulated stucco finish.

Insulating Masonry Walls—Interior

Depending on the condition of the walls and the insulation used, interior masonry walls can be insulated in several ways. Rigid board insulation can be bonded directly to even, plumb masonry walls. Uneven walls can be furred out with furring strips to ensure an even bonding surface. Extremely uneven walls or irregular stone walls may require a framework of 2" by 4" lumber with fiberglass batt or blanket insulation installed within this wall cavity. Before beginning any of these insulation methods, always be sure to solve any moisture problems your basement or below-grade wall may have.

Rigid Board Insulation—Even Walls. Before insulating a masonry wall with rigid board insulation, be sure that the surface to which you will be bonding is

structurally sound, clean, dry, and free of grease and loose paint. Poured concrete foundations are often coated with a film of oil, grease, or silicone used as a
mold release when the foundation was formed. These substances inhibit bonding and must be removed with a wash of trisodium phosphate (TSP) or a strong
detergent before applying any adhesive.

If the masonry wall is even and plumb, furring strips will not be necessary. To
begin the installation, remove all baseboards and other trim. Using an appropri-
ate construction adhesive and masonry nails, glue and nail horizontal wood
strips (2" wide and the same thickness as the foam insulation) continuously
along the top and bottom edges of the masonry walls and around windows and
doors (Fig. 11-10). Cut the rigid board insulation to fit around all surface projections, such as windows, wood strips, electrical outlets, and conduits. This is
accomplished easily with a sharp utility knife by scoring the insulation and
snapping it or by cutting all the way through it.

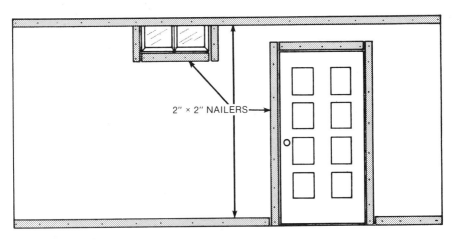

*Fig. 11-10: Attach nailers along the top and bottom of the wall and around any windows,
doors, etc.*

After referring to the instructions on the adhesive cartridge for any specific
directions, apply a continuous bead of panel and foam adhesive around the
perimeter of the rigid board insulation. Also apply strips of adhesive to the center
of the boards. As an alternate application method, apply golf-ball-sized globs of
adhesive on 12" centers around the perimeter and across the surface of the
board. **CAUTION:** Before applying any adhesive on rigid board polystyrene
insulation, make absolutely certain that the adhesive is formulated for this
purpose. Special panel and foam adhesives are available for safely bonding this
type of insulation. As stated earlier in this book, polystyrene can be severely
damaged by certain solvents contained in many adhesive formulations.

Glue and install one panel at a time. When the adhesive has been applied,
place the insulation board against the wall surface either horizontally or vertically, depending on which position is more practical. Uniformly press the board to
the wall surface to ensure a positive and intimate bond (Fig. 11-11A). Make any
necessary adjustments before the adhesive sets. Repeat this action for every
board.

Do not insulate over water or drain pipes. Instead, butt the insulation up to the pipes and, if possible, wedge some insulation behind the pipes. During the winter months, heat from the interior of the house may be necessary to prevent pipes from freezing and bursting.

Allow the adhesive to dry for 24 hours before covering the insulation with any other finishing materials. If the walls are poured concrete instead of concrete block, allow several days for the adhesive to dry. In some cases where the concrete is extremely nonporous, the adhesive may take as long as 30 days to adequately dry. Test the bond by trying to pull a piece of insulation from the wall.

One-half inch drywall is a popular finish material to place over rigid-board-insulated masonry walls. A panel and foam adhesive and drywall nails are used to attach the drywall to the nailers and the insulation. First, extrude the panel and foam adhesive to the back of the drywall in the same manner as described previously for the rigid board insulation. Bond the drywall to the wall by applying uniform pressure to all areas of the drywall, and complete fastening by nailing on 6" centers along the top and bottom nailers (Fig. 11-11B) and around windows and doors. To finish the job, compound, tape, sand, and paint the drywall.

A   B

Fig. 11-11: (A) Press insulation against masonry wall and (B) nail drywall on 6" centers.

Rigid Board Insulation—Uneven Walls. On uneven walls or walls that are more than 1/4" out of plumb, furring strips must be used to create a flat gluing and nailing base for the finishing material; the finishing material must always be placed over the rigid board insulation. The actual rigid board insulation is placed between the furring strips.

Precut furring strips can be obtained from your lumber dealer, or you can make your own by ripping 2" by 4" stock into 2" by 2" strips. Use only dry, straight furring to ensure a smooth, flat wall.

A combination of vertical and horizontal furring strips are used (Fig. 11-12A). Begin by bonding horizontal nailers along the top and bottom of the wall and by bonding vertical nailers (2 by 4s) in each corner. Bond them to the walls with a construction adhesive. Apply 1/4" diameter beads in a serpentine pattern across the back side of each nailer and 2 by 4. Press them firmly against the wall until the adhesive holds.

Attach the vertical strips next. Apply a 1/4" diameter bead in a serpentine pattern to each strip. Press the strips to the wall on 4' centers. Use a carpenter's level to check for plumbness. Press the strips firmly into place. Where the strips are not flat against the wall, use a short piece of shingle as a shim or filler (Fig. 11-12B). Following the same procedures, install horizontal strips on 16" centers between the vertical strips.

Using a utility knife, score and break the rigid board insulation into sizes that will fit between the furring strips. Bond the insulation to the masonry wall with a panel and foam adhesive. Apply the adhesive in 1/4" diameter beads around the perimeters of the boards and in an "X" pattern across the panel centers. Glue one board at a time, pressing the boards firmly to the wall.

The band joists should also be insulated at this time. Use a blanket insulation with a vapor barrier facing. Cut the insulation into sections slightly larger than the cavity formed by the floor joists and band joists. With vapor barrier facing in toward the basement, staple the facing flange to the sides of the joists. Peel the facing away from the top and bottom of the insulation, and staple the facing to the subfloor and to the top furring strip (Fig. 11-12C). The band joist that runs parallel to the floor joist must be insulated in a similar fashion. Staple the vapor barrier to the subfloor and the top furring strip. Tape the seams where separate

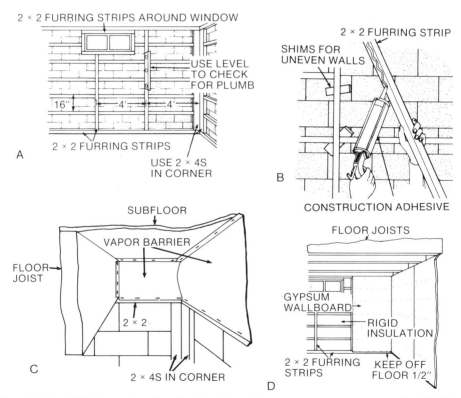

Fig. 11-12: (A) Horizontal and vertical furring strips over uneven masonry walls. (B) Shim where necessary to create an even surface. (C) Staple faced fiberglass insulation to the band joist. (D) Install drywall over insulation and nailers.

lengths of insulation meet with duct tape. Remember that if moisture seeps behind the insulation and condenses, it could result in the formation of mildew and dry rot.

One-half inch drywall makes an excellent fire-rated finishing material for this installation. The drywall is installed with adhesive and nails as shown in Fig. 11-12D. Because the floor in a basement is often sloped for drainage purposes, it is extremely important that you accurately measure the wall height as you proceed. Cut the bottom of each drywall sheet to conform to the slope of the floor, sizing each sheet 1/2" shorter than the floor to ceiling joist height.

To install a sheet of drywall, apply a 1/4" diameter bead of drywall adhesive to the furring strips in a serpentine fashion. Use only enough adhesive to bond one panel at a time. Set each sheet of drywall on 1/2" blocks and press the panel against the wall, applying pressure over every square foot of drywall. Drive several nails into the top and bottom strips to hold the drywall in place until the adhesive sets. Wait 24 hours before spackling and finishing the wall.

Fig. 11-13: A framed masonry wall.

Batt and Blanket Insulation—Framed Walls. Batt and blanket insulation may also be used to insulate a masonry wall once a frame constructed of 2" by 4" lumber has been built over the wall (Fig. 11-13). Framing the wall is not a difficult task because the frame can be assembled on the floor and simply stood in place for final nailing.

If you wish to insulate masonry walls in this manner, begin by measuring the distance from the floor to the ceiling joists. Cut the 2" by 4" studs to a length dimension 3-1/2" shorter than this height dimension. These 3-1/2" allow for top and bottom sills (each 1-1/2" high) and 1/2" clearance when the frame is stood in place.

Mark the location of the studs on the top and bottom sill pieces, spacing the studs on 16" centers. Nail the studs to the sills with 10d nails. Once all studs are nailed, stand the finished frame against the masonry wall and place 1/2" wood shims beneath the bottom sill to raise the frame up against the joists overhead. Use a level to check for plumbness. Nail the top sill to the overhead joists using 16d nails, and secure the bottom sill to the basement floor by extruding construction adhesive between the sill and floor. It is also a good practice to extrude a serpentine bead onto the floor before raising the frame into position.

After the frame is up and secured, the wall can be insulated with batts or blankets as described in the section "Installing Batt or Blanket Insulation—New Construction" found earlier in this chapter. It is not necessary to cover the entire wall with insulation. The insulation should extend from the top of the wall down to a point 2' below grade. It is necessary, though, to cover the entire wall with a vapor barrier in order to prevent condensation on the masonry wall. If faced batts or blankets cover the entire wall, the need for a vapor barrier will be satisfied.

The framed wall must not be left unfinished since most vapor barriers on batt and blanket insulation are combustible. Hardboard is an excellent choice for finishing framed-out basement walls.

Hardboard specially manufactured for use as prefinished paneling is specifically treated for resistance to stains, scrubbing, and moisture. It is also highly resistant to dents, mars, and scuffs. In most cases, the material is prefinished in wood grains such as walnut, cherry, birch, oak, teak, and pecan and in a variety of shades. It may be smooth surfaced or random grooved. In addition there are the decorative and work-saving plastic-surfaced hardboards that resist water, stains, and household chemicals exceptionally well. A typical surface consists of baked-on plastic. Most hardboard is sufficiently dense and moisture-resistant for use in bathrooms, kitchens, laundry rooms, and basements. The variety of finishes and sizes is extensive. Finishes include rich-looking wood grains, exceptional marble reproductions, plain colors, speckled colors, simulated tile, lace prints, wallpaper textures, and murals. Vinyl-clad panels are also available in decorative and wood grain finishes.

Use 3/16", 1/4", and 5/16" hardboard over open framing. All panel edges should fall on studs. Remember, as mentioned previously, framing studs should be spaced no more than 16" on center.

Make sure that all surfaces to which adhesive is to be applied are clean and dry. Then apply a 1/8" thick continuous ribbon of adhesive to studs, or other surfaces to which panel edges are to be bonded (Fig. 11-14A). If vertical and horizontal furring strips are being used as backing in a paneling installation, then apply an intermittent ribbon (3" bead, 6" open space) to intermediate furring (Fig. 11-14B). Adhesive and room temperatures should be between 60°F and 100°F during application.

Move the panel into position over studs or furring strips and immediately press into place (Fig. 11-14C). Install two nails at the top of the panel to maintain its position, leaving the heads exposed for subsequent easy removal (Fig. 11-14D). With uniform hand pressure, press the panels firmly into contact with the adhesive bead (Fig. 11-14E). Carefully remove the nails, protecting the panel surface with a scrap of carpeting (Fig. 11-14F).

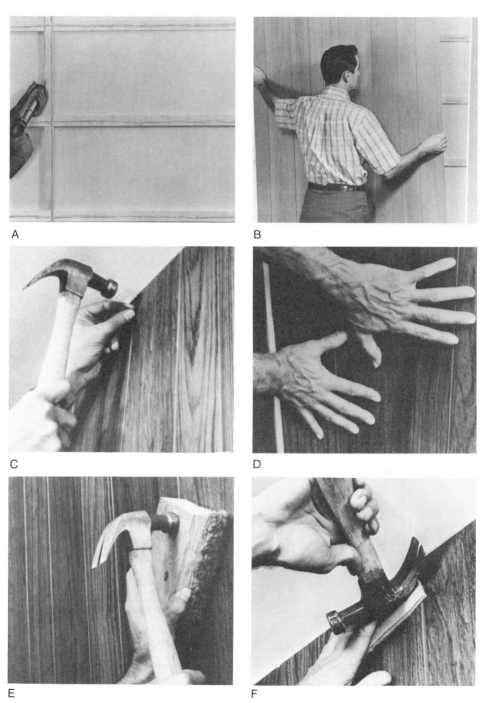

A

B

C

D

E

F

Fig. 11-14: Apply hardboard paneling over a stud or furring strip frame.

Insulating Masonry Walls with Metal Furring

Masonry walls having metal furring strips should be insulated with rigid board insulation (Fig. 11-15). The metal strips are attached to the wall with concrete anchoring bolts or panel and metal framing adhesive, and as with wooden furring, the rigid board insulation fits between the furring strips. The metal Z-channels are installed on 24" centers. If the insulation is sufficiently thick, the furring will hold it in place with a friction fit. If not, a panel and foam adhesive should be used to bond the insulation to the wall. Extrude globs of adhesive about the size of golf balls every 12" across the boards and press each firmly into place.

To finish the job, attach drywall to the metal furring strips using a metal framing construction adhesive. Extrude a 1/4" diameter bead of adhesive to the face of each metal furring strip and press the drywall paneling against the furring. Support the drywall panel until the adhesive sets. After the adhesive is dry, the drywall can be taped, spackled, sanded, and painted.

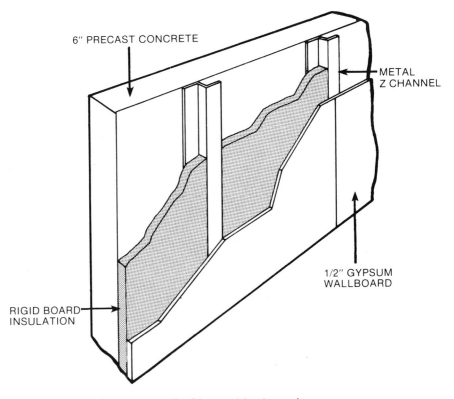

Fig. 11-15: Insulated masonry wall with metal furring strips.

Insulating Foundations 12

Three types of foundations are used in residential buildings: full basement, crawl space, and slab-on-grade. Each should be insulated against heat loss and sealed against moisture invasion.

INSULATING AN UNHEATED BASEMENT

Placing insulation on the interior masonry walls of an unheated basement is neither necessary nor desirable, since it would merely divide the unheated ground from the unheated basement. Remember, the purpose of insulation is the separation of unheated areas from heated areas. Instead, the insulation should be placed in the floor joists above the basement area, to separate it from the heated living space above.

Do not place insulation in a heated basement's ceiling if you plan to renovate the basement into a living area or if your furnace and hot water heater are in the basement. Doing so will waste heat through the concrete walls. For example, many homeowners are placing wood and coal stoves in their basements to mitigate the escalating cost of heating. If a basement ceiling is insulated, the supplemental heat will be trapped in the basement and will escape through the concrete walls. Very little of it will work its way up into living spaces where it could help lower heating costs. The same principle applies to primary furnaces and water heaters. Wasted heat from these appliances will not work up to the living spaces if the ceiling is insulated.

Choosing Insulation for Basement Ceilings

The types of insulation suitable for insulating a basement ceiling are limited by the force of gravity. Obviously, loose-fill materials cannot be installed. Foams and spray-on cellulose are also difficult for the homeowner to install overhead. That leaves rigid board and batt or blanket insulation. The usual choice is fiberglass batts. Floor joists are normally installed 16" or 24" on center, and batts fit snugly into the intervening spaces. If the joists are spaced unevenly, cut the batts 1/2" wider than joist spaces.

Installing Basement Ceiling Insulation

Use unfaced insulation (Fig. 12-1), and press the insulation against the flooring overhead. Do not leave an air space between the flooring and the insulation. If you do, air movement will permit the heat to bypass the insulation. A vapor barrier between the overhead floor and the insulation is unnecessary. The temperature in the basement is tempered by the temperature of the soil so that the dew point normally will not be reached inside the insulation.

Fig. 12-1: Place unfaced batt or blanket insulation in the basement ceiling.

If you do use fiberglass insulation with a vapor barrier facing, install the insulation with the vapor barrier pressed against the flooring. Do not reverse the insulation and staple the vapor barrier to the floor joists. Doing so will trap water vapor inside the insulation, where it will reduce the thermal resistance of the insulation. The stapling flange is not designed to support the insulation and will eventually pull loose from the staples. Instead, one of the methods of securing the insulation shown in Fig. 12-2 should be used.

The surest method of supporting the insulation is to use chicken wire mesh. But, wire mesh is expensive, difficult with which to work, and can only be used when the insulation is as thick as the depth of the joists. Use 2" mesh, and staple it to the joists.

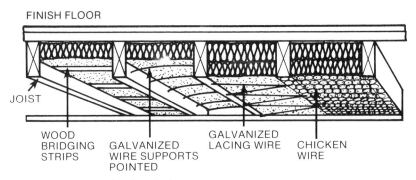

Fig. 12-2: Ways of securing insulation.

Nylon string or wire is cheaper and easier to use. Staple the wire to the sides of the joists in a zigzag pattern. Nails can also be driven at intervals into the joists, and the wire can then be strung between the nails in a shoestring fashion.

Wood strapping can be used to hold the insulation in the ceiling if the insulation fills the joist space. Simply nail the strapping across the joists. Ceiling tile can be attached to the nailers if a finished ceiling is desired.

If the thickness of the insulation is less than the depth of the joists, heavy galvanized wires can be used to hold the insulation up against the flooring. Purchase 15" or 23" lengths of the wires from an insulation supplier. The ends of the wires are sharpened so that the wires, when pushed up between the joists, embed in the sides of the joists and hold firmly.

INSULATING THE EXTERIOR FOUNDATION

If your basement is heated, one of the least expensive ways to insulate the foundation is to attach rigid board insulation to the exterior perimeter. There are many positive aspects to placing insulation on the exterior rather than the interior of your foundation, whether it is slab, crawl space, or basement. A major advantage is the capacity of the *thermal mass* of the concrete to actually conserve heat better than R-values indicate. Although the R-value per inch of a poured concrete or block wall is very low, the masonry also acts like a sponge to store heat; therefore, room temperatures are more stable in both winter and summer. Insulation placed on the interior walls negates any thermal stability that might be derived from the masonry.

Another advantage is that insulation placed on the exterior surface of your foundation wall does not take up space inside the basement where space is already limited. Nor will the insulation on the exterior wall present the fire hazard that it does inside the basement. Exterior insulation will not require furring or studs and does not need to be covered with expensive wall finishes such as drywall or wood paneling.

There are still more benefits derived from insulating outside walls: Properly installed insulation will funnel rainwater away from the basement walls, thus eliminating aggravating water problems in your basement. Insulation on the exterior will also reduce the danger of frost damage to your foundation. Cold will be prevented from penetrating beyond the insulation, and the chance of buckling and heaving of the foundation will be less than if you insulated the interior walls.

Installing Rigid Board to Exterior Foundation

Placing insulation on the exterior surfaces may be the best way to insulate a foundation, but it also means a lot of work. A trench 12" to 18" deep and 2' to 3' wide must be dug around the foundation, and a cementitious coating must be troweled over the above-grade portion of the insulation to protect it against the harmful rays of the sun (Fig. 12-3). In many parts of the country, this type of work cannot be done during the cold winter months when the ground is frozen.

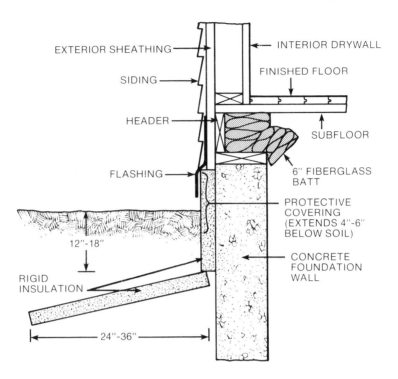

Fig. 12-3: Details of exterior foundation insulation.

If you decide to insulate your foundation's exterior, first call your utility companies and have service representatives point out where the utility lines enter your house. Most utility lines are either overhead or buried deeper than you will have to dig, but it is always wise to be sure before doing any excavating.

Depending on the depth of frost in your area, dig the trench 12" to 18" deep and 2' wide, as previously mentioned. Do not dig more than you can insulate in a day or weekend. An unexpected rainstorm will leave water standing against your basement walls. Use a cement patching compound to fill any cracks that you discover in the foundation.

Next, apply the vertical layer of tongue-and-groove insulation. Extrude a panel and foam adhesive in strips spaced 12" apart to the back of the rigid board. Press the boards firmly against the wall.

A protective covering must be placed over the insulation at this point. Apply a latex foam or cement-based covering or stucco over the insulation to protect it from the sun. This protection should extend 4" to 6" below grade. If for some reason you are not able to apply a protective covering immediately, cover the insulation with polyethylene.

With the vertical portion of the foundation insulation installed, grade the trench so that it slopes away from the wall. Lay the horizontal layer of insulation so that it butts tightly against the wall and the bottom of the vertical insulation. Then drape 6-mil polyethylene sheeting over the vertical and horizontal boards so that rainwater will not seep down between the joints. Overlap successive sheets of the plastic at least 6". Backfill over the insulation and grade the soil to slope away from the house. This will further help to channel water away from your basement walls.

The last step is to install flashing over the top of the insulation. Push aluminum or galvanized steel flashing up under the lower two courses of siding material and shape the flashing to fit over the top of the insulation. An upside-down J-channel may also be used as shown in Fig. 12-4. Also, if the insulation does not extend up over the header, insulate this area from the inside with faced fiberglass.

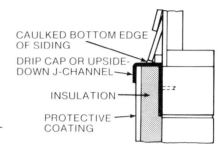

CAULKED BOTTOM EDGE OF SIDING

DRIP CAP OR UPSIDE-DOWN J-CHANNEL

INSULATION

PROTECTIVE COATING

Fig. 12-4: Flashing and coating protect foundation insulation from moisture.

INSULATING CRAWL SPACES

Crawl spaces present some unique insulating problems. Besides having masonry walls that offer little resistance to heat loss, crawl spaces usually have dirt floors, which allow moisture to seep into the crawl space area. If this moisture is not eliminated, the performance of any insulation placed in the crawl space will be impaired.

Crawl spaces also have a problem with cold air infiltration. All crawl spaces must be ventilated during the summer months to help dispel moisture. During the winter months when the relative humidity is much lower, moisture is no longer a problem, but improperly sealed vents can allow cold air to continually pass through the crawl space and remove heat from the heated areas above.

Insulating Unheated Crawl Spaces

An uninsulated crawl space should be insulated in much the same way as an unheated basement. Fiberglass batts or blankets should be placed between the floor joists in the ceiling as shown in Fig. 12-5. However, instead of unfaced

Fig. 12-5: Install fiberglass batts or blankets against the subfloor in a crawl space ceiling.

insulation, batts or blankets with attached vapor barriers should be used. Place the insulation between the joists with the vapor barrier pressed against the subfloor above it. Attach the insulation in place by using one of the methods described earlier in this chapter under the heading, "Insulating an Unheated Basement." Figure 12-6 illustrates insulation held in place with chicken wire—an easy, popular attachment method.

If the insulation does not completely fill the joist space, it is important that you fill the band joist cavity with insulation. This prevents air movement above the insulation, and the dead air space between the insulation and the subfloor adds to the R-value of the floor, especially if the insulation has a foil vapor barrier facing.

To complete the installation, place a layer of 6-mil polyethylene sheeting over the dirt floor of the crawl space. Cover the entire floor, overlapping the edges of adjacent sheets 6" or more. Tape all seams with duct tape, and be sure to tape the edges of the sheets to the crawl space walls.

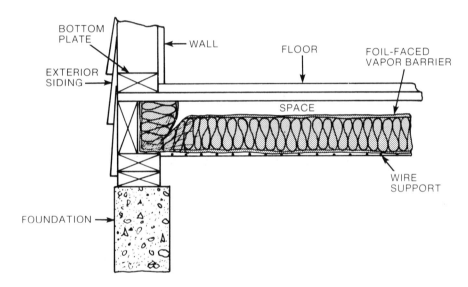

Fig. 12-6: Foil insulation and a dead air space increase the insulative effect of crawl space ceiling insulation.

Insulating Heated Crawl Spaces

If your home has a forced air heating system and warm, conditioned air moves through the crawl space area, insulation should be placed on the walls of the area instead of between the joists above it. This is also true if heat sources, such as furnaces or water heaters, are located in the crawl space area. Insulation on the walls will prevent warm air or wasted heat from escaping through the foundation. Heat in the crawl space will help warm the floor area above it. Fiberglass batts or blankets or rigid board polystyrene insulation can be used.

When using fiberglass insulation, utilize unfaced blankets, and cut the blankets to length so that they extend from the top of the band joist to a point 2' over the floor perimeter. Stuff the band joist cavity with short lengths of insulation (Fig. 12-7A), and attach the long length of the blanket by nailing it to the sill plate with 1/2" by 1-1/2" nailers as shown in Fig. 12-7B. Fit the blankets snugly against each other and secure the blankets at the base of the wall by laying a piece of lumber on the edge of the blankets (Fig. 12-7C).

Applying rigid board insulation is an alternate treatment for heated crawl spaces (Fig. 12-8). Rigid board insulation used in crawl space applications does not require a fire-retardant covering if all of the following conditions are met:

1. Entry to the crawl space is made only for service or maintenance.
2. There are no interconnected basement areas.
3. Air in the crawl space is not circulated to other parts of the building.

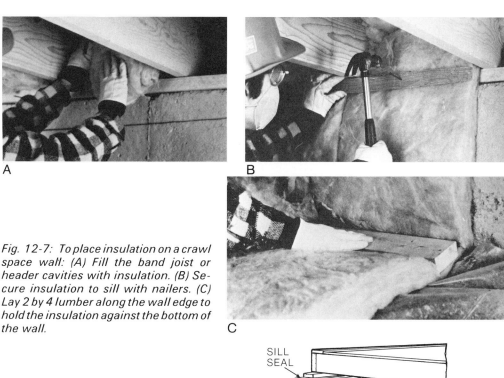

Fig. 12-7: To place insulation on a crawl space wall: (A) Fill the band joist or header cavities with insulation. (B) Secure insulation to sill with nailers. (C) Lay 2 by 4 lumber along the wall edge to hold the insulation against the bottom of the wall.

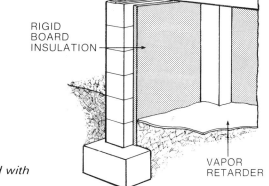

SILL
SEAL

RIGID
BOARD
INSULATION

VAPOR
RETARDER

Fig. 12-8: A crawl space insulated with rigid board insulation.

Begin the installation by digging down to the footing along the crawl space walls. Scrape dirt and burrs from the masonry surface with a wire brush, and stuff fiberglass insulation into the band joist cavity areas. Cut the rigid polystyrene board to fit the entire masonry wall. Fasten the panels to the wall with a panel and foam adhesive specially formulated to bond polystyrene to masonry surfaces. Extrude the adhesive in a continuous strip across the back of a rigid board. Press the board to the wall, applying pressure over every square foot of the surface area. Brace the board in place until the adhesive sets. Follow this procedure for each board until the entire crawl space wall is insulated.

Ventilating to Control Ground Moisture. Regardless of the insulation used on the walls, ground moisture must be controlled in heated crawl spaces. Lay 6-mil polyethylene sheeting over the floor, and tape all seams tight. Secure the edges of the sheeting to the crawl space walls with duct tape. To allow moisture to escape instead of condensing on the underflooring above, foundation ventilators or masonry ventilators must be installed.

The basementless crawl spaces should have a net free ventilated area of 1/150 of the ground area except when the ground surface is covered with a vapor barrier. If a vapor barrier is used, the ratio can be reduced to 1/1500.

During the winter months, seal vents tightly to keep out the cold air. You can make a tight-fitting vent cover yourself (Fig. 12-9). Construct the covers with lattice or molding and polyethylene plastic. Make the frame large enough to completely cover the vent opening. Cut a sheet of polyethylene 1" longer and 1" wider than the frame, and fold the plastic over the frame, stapling it to the sides of the frame. Attach the frame to the foundation or siding with an acrylic latex caulk. Because acrylic latex caulks are water-based and, thus, dry slowly, devise a way to hold the frame in place until the caulk dries. Once dry, the latex caulk will hold the cover in place during the winter months. In the spring, simply pry off the cover of the vent opening to break the caulk seal and free the cover.

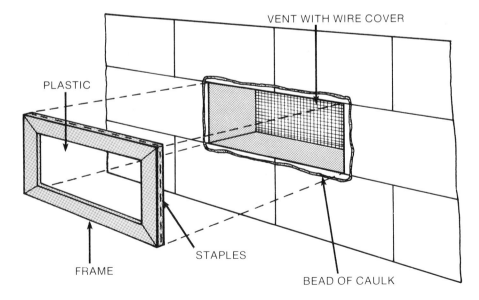

Fig. 12-9: A crawl space vent cover.

INSULATING SLAB-ON-GRADE FOUNDATIONS

A slab floor foundation can be insulated in several ways. Exterior rigid board insulation, described earlier in the section entitled, "Insulating the Exterior Foundation," is also applicable for slab-on-grade foundations. The insulation should extend from the top of the slab down to the footing (Fig. 12-10). After backfilling, be sure to apply a protective covering to any exposed portions of the insulation.

Another way to insulate a slab floor is to place rigid board insulation between the slab floor and sleepers (Fig. 12-11). The insulation and sleepers are then covered with a subfloor and the floor is finished with carpet, tile, etc. Before applying the insulation board, be sure the floor surface to which you will be

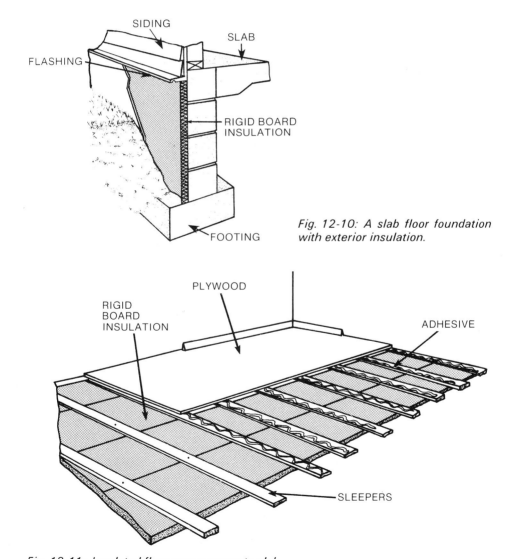

Fig. 12-10: A slab floor foundation with exterior insulation.

Fig. 12-11: Insulated floor over a concrete slab.

bonding the board is structurally sound, clean, dry, and free of oil and loose paint. Any cracks should be filled with patching cement or a suitable concrete latex underlayment several days prior to installation. If your concrete floor has a drain, you will probably not want to cover the drain, unless you can determine that your local code allows it to be covered.

Determine in which direction the subfloor panels should run and plan to run the sleepers at right angles to the subfloor panels. Using a chalk line, strike a series of lines 16" on center beginning at the wall that will run perpendicular to the direction of your subfloor panel installation. Apply a serpentine bead of good quality construction adhesive over each chalk line and lay 2 by 2 lumber (treated with preservatives) on these beads. If heating coils are in the slab, make sure that the adhesives will tolerate the temperatures that may be reached.

When the sleepers are installed, cut rigid board insulation to fit between the sleepers. Place a continuous bead of foam adhesive around the perimeter of each insulation board, as well as an x-shaped deposit from corner to corner. Cut each board as necessary to fit around posts, doors, pipes, etc. Make sure that each board fits tightly against the preceding ones.

OTHER VENTILATION NEEDS

Wall condensation problems occur when moisture vapor inside the house seeps into the hollow spaces in the walls. This moisture works its way through to the outside walls and pushes exterior paint away from the siding, causing blisters and peeling. Paint breather vents or miniature circular louvered vents are employed to correct this problem. These vents are easily installed between the stud spaces, by simply drilling a hole the diameter of the vent and tapping the vent into place. Installation of vents near the lower and upper part of the outside wall provide an intake and an outlet ventilation system.

The laundry area is another major source of humidity. The best solution in this problem area is to vent the dryer to the outside and to install an exhaust fan near the washing machine. Installation kits are available which contain everything needed to vent a clothes dryer plus complete instructions for doing the job. The new, smooth flow flexible duct makes the job of installing ventilating exhaust fans much easier, too.

Insulating Steel Buildings 13

Steel buildings are growing in popularity today. For many years steel construction was confined to industrial and commercial buildings where strength was the predominant factor in the choice of building materials. After a decade and a half of rising lumber prices and energy costs, many builders are now turning to steel as a low-cost, energy-efficient alternative to wood frame construction (Fig. 13-1).

Fig. 13-1: A steel building.

Steel has many advantages over wood frame construction. For example, steel does not decay, is impervious to water, will not support combustion, requires little maintenance if properly coated, and most importantly, has mechanical strength properties far superior to wood framing members. The strength of the steel framing members permits fewer pieces to be used, resulting in reduced material costs, labor costs, and erection time. That translates into substantial savings.

Properly designed and insulated, a steel building can be very energy efficient. Some steel buildings permit extra thicknesses of insulation in walls and roof. Superinsulated frames with active and passive solar features are common in steel building designs. Techniques for insulating metal framed walls and ceilings are explained in the following pages.

145

INSULATING ON-BEAM STEEL BUILDINGS

On-beam construction commonly utilizes steel beams spaced as much as 6' on center. The wide spacing and simple framing arrangement permits fast erection of the building frame with a substantial savings in labor and materials. The large framing members also permit installation of insulation in great thicknesses. Ten inches of fiberglass insulation with an R-value of 33 is possible.

Insulating with Fiberglass Batts or Blankets

Figure 13-2 illustrates a steel building insulated with fiberglass batts. The steel beams are spaced 6' on center. Metal siding is fixed to the exterior and 2 by 4 furring strips are fastened to the inside. Unfaced fiberglass blankets or batts fill the cavity between the beams, and a vapor barrier of 4 mil polyethylene plastic is stapled over the furring strips.

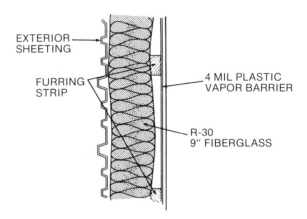

EXTERIOR SHEETING

FURRING STRIP

4 MIL PLASTIC VAPOR BARRIER

R-30 9" FIBERGLASS

Fig. 13-2: Insulated walls in steel building.

Keeping the insulation in place may be difficult. The width of the frame spacing requires placing three blankets side by side. Fiberglass batts with a kraft facing and tabs cannot be stapled to the framing like they can in wood frame walls. Another means must be used to keep the three blankets per cavity in place until the finish wall material is installed. A quick-grabbing contact cement such as contact-bond adhesive will hold the unfaced batts in place until the finish wall material is installed. Spray or brush the cement over the metal siding. After letting the adhesive air for a few minutes (see manufacturer's instructions for drying times), press the insulation in place. Momentary pressure will bond the fiberglass to the siding long enough to install the finish wall material. Be sure to fill the cavity between the beams completely with insulation.

Careful installation of the vapor barrier is important. Moisture drastically reduces the insulating value of fiberglass batts. The sheets of polyethylene must completely cover the insulated walls. Overlap adjacent sheets by several inches. Staple the sheet to the furring strips every 2". Do not create puckers in the plastic edge that would allow air to bypass the vapor barrier.

Insulating with Rigid Board Insulation

Boxing steel beams with rough hewn cedar gives a rustic look to any room. To achieve this effect, insulation and finish wall material must be placed between the beams (Fig. 13-3). Again, attaching insulation and wall material to the metal siding is a problem. Mechanical fasteners are unsuitable; therefore, an adhesive is recommended. Many adhesives are unsuitable for bonding rigid board insulation to metal. As has been previously stated, the solvents in many adhesives—including neoprene-type panel and metal framing adhesives—attack polystyrene and other rigid board insulation products. Other adhesives do not have the temperature resistance to withstand the high temperatures often encountered in metal buildings. Still other adhesives dry slowly when sandwiched between two nonporous surfaces such as metal siding and polystyrene.

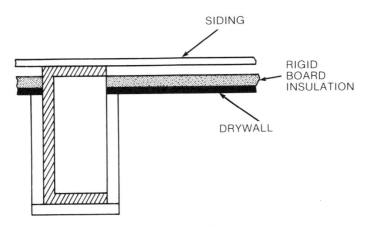

Fig. 13-3: Rigid board insulation between structural beams.

The best choice of adhesives when applying rigid board insulation to metal surfaces is a neoprene contact cement such as rubber-based contact bond adhesive. When brushed on both the metal siding and the rigid board insulation, the adhesive develops excellent bonding strength and temperature resistance.

To install rigid board insulation between the beams in on-beam construction homes, you must first cut the 4' by 8' sheets to size. If the beams are spaced 6' on center, you will need one-and-a-half sheets per section.

Next, brush the contact cement on the siding and on one side of the insulation. Carefully follow the manufacturer's instructions concerning application, drying times, and ventilation. Usually the manufacturer suggests waiting up to an hour before placing the two surfaces together. This allows some of the water to evaporate and increases the initial grab.

Carefully position the sheet of insulation before pressing it in place. Once the two tacky surfaces make contact, they cannot be separated.

Allow ample time for the adhesive to dry before applying finish wall material. Depending on weather conditions, it may take days or even weeks for the water-based adhesive to dry completely. Of course, you can test the bond strength at any time by just trying to pull the insulation away from the siding.

INSULATING LIGHTWEIGHT STEEL FRAME BUILDINGS

Many steel buildings are being built today with specially designed steel components called "Super C" studs and joists. Construction is similar to wood stud frame constructions (Fig. 13-4). Studs and joists are spaced 16" or 24" on center and insulation is easily installed in the cavity-type walls and ceilings.

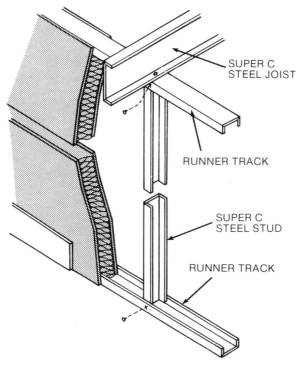

Fig. 13-4: "Super C" steel framing.

Insulating Exterior Steel Frame Walls

The only difference between insulating a wood stud wall or ceiling and a steel stud wall or ceiling is the method of attachment. Wall cavities can be filled with unfaced fiberglass batts. The width of the batt or blanket is usually slightly larger than the cavity; thus, the compression fit should hold the insulation in place. If, for any reason, this is not the case, spray or brush a contact cement over the exterior siding. As already explained in the previous section, by pressing the fiberglass against the adhesive, the insulation will be bonded to the siding.

Attaching a vapor barrier is another problem. One solution is to finish the wall with foil-backed gypsum wallboard. The aluminum foil is an excellent vapor barrier. Seal the edges of the 4' by 8' sheets by extruding panel and metal framing adhesive over the steel studs and runner tracks (Fig. 13-5). Extrude a serpentine bead on beams on which a panel edge does not fall. On studs where panel edges meet, extrude a double bead of adhesive.

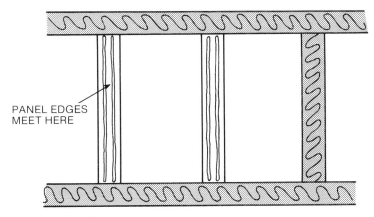

PANEL EDGES
MEET HERE

Fig. 13-5: Extruding adhesive to steel framing.

Cut the drywall panels to size and power-nail them to the studs. The adhesive will not only help to seal the edges of the foil-backed wall boards, but will also add to the rigidity of the building frame.

Insulating Interior Steel Frame Walls

Fiberglass insulation is often added to interior walls to lessen sound transmission. In this case, vapor barriers are unnecessary and adhesives can be used to attach paneling or drywall directly to the studs.

Extrude a 1/4" bead of panel and metal frame adhesive in a serpentine fashion over the face of each stud. Cut the panels to size and press into position. Attach the top of each panel to the horizontal runner track with three self-tapping screws. With a padded block and a hammer, tap the panels over each stud to press the panels into the adhesive. Finish the installation by attaching the bottom of each panel to the bottom runner track with three self-tapping screws.

After one side of the interior wall is finished with paneling, fiberglass acoustical insulation can be glued in the cavities to the back of the paneling. The other side of the wall can then be paneled in the manner just described.

INSULATING METAL BUILDINGS WITH SPINDLE ANCHORS

Not all steel structures lend themselves well to the techniques just described. For example, metal buildings used as garages, workshops, or storage shelters often require insulation, but a finished interior wall is not always necessary in such cases. These buildings are often pole frame buildings with metal siding.

A common way of insulating this type of building is to drape the walls and ceiling with vinyl-faced fiberglass blankets. But because finish wall material will not be installed over the insulation, another means of keeping it in place must be found.

Metal roofs are another area where installing insulation can be a problem. In steel buildings, roof insulation is usually laid between ceiling joists or held between rafters by furring strips. Other situations where finished ceiling materials are not installed require other means of securing the insulation.

An excellent way for the do-it-yourselfer to fasten insulation in applications where other fasteners are not suitable is with spindle anchors (Fig. 13-6). Available at your nearest home supply center, spindle anchors have a perforated base from the center of which protrudes a long spindle.

To install insulation with spindle anchors, first use a putty knife to place a blob of adhesive on the spindle base (Fig. 13-6A). The proper adhesive is usually supplied by the spindle anchor manufacturer. Next, press the spindle anchor onto the surface over which the insulation must be placed (Fig. 13-6B). Twist it to evenly distribute the adhesive under the base. Then, let the adhesive dry. Install enough spindles over the wall surface to support the insulation. When the adhesive is dry (usually within 24 to 48 hours), impale the insulation on the spindles. Place self-locking washers over the spindles and bend the ends of the spindles over (Fig. 13-6C).

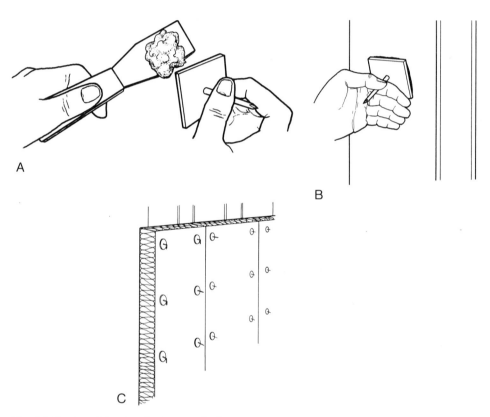

Fig. 13-6: Attaching insulation to spindle anchors: (A) Apply adhesive to anchor; (B) press anchor into position; and (C) hang insulation on spindle.

Other
Energy-Saving 14
Techniques

In the preceding chapters, you were presented with a variety of ways to conserve energy in your home. By insulating, caulking, and weatherstripping, you can take a healthy bite out of your heating/cooling costs. But don't quit now. You don't have to be satisfied with just a 20% or 30% reduction in your utility/ fuel bills. There are many other energy conservation techniques that you can use to slash away at the cost of keeping your home comfortable. A few of the most money-wise techniques are given in this chapter.

UTILIZING ENERGY-EFFICIENT WINDOWS

A single pane of glass has an R-value of 0.88 to 0.91 as compared to a typical insulated 2 by 4 frame wall with an R-value of 14.41. Heat passes very readily— almost eagerly—through the windows of your house. A simple test will demonstrate this phenomenon dramatically. On a cold day, hold the palm of your hand as close to a window as possible without touching it. Almost immediately your hand will feel colder. This sensation is the result of the speed with which the window absorbs heat from your hand. Now, hold your hand close to an insulated wall. Feel the difference? Unless you do something to improve the R-value of the glass area in your home, 20% to 30% of the cost of heating and cooling will literally go out the window.

Installing Storm Windows

There are many ways to stop winter heat loss through windows. Shutters, quilted shades, heavy drapes, and cornices are just some of the commonly used heat stoppers. The best solution to energy loss through cold windows is storm windows. Storm windows create an additional still air space that adds to the insulative value of a window. Storm windows also reduce infiltration of cold air around window rails, stiles, jambs, casing, sills, and glazing.

You can build storm windows with wood furring strips, angle irons, and sheet plastic or acrylic. A wood frame is easy to make. Simply measure for the mounting position of the storm window and cut the furring strips to size. Miter the ends of each piece 45° and connect the frame pieces with angle irons (Fig. 14-1A). Before screwing the angle irons to the frame, predrill with a bit slightly smaller than the diameter of the screws. Predrilling will prevent the screws from splitting the 1 by 3s. Paint the frame to protect it from moisture.

Attach sheet vinyl or sheet plastic with tacks, staples, or nails. For a tighter fit, tack nailer strips over the edge of the plastic (Fig. 14-1B). If acrylic is used, screw it tightly into place against the frame.

Attach foam weatherstripping to the back of the frame and screw the frame into place with long galvanized or brass screws (Fig. 14-1C). Or attach hanging brackets, which will make seasonal installation and removal easy. With acrylic latex caulk, seal any gaps between the frame and the house to ensure an airtight air space between the primary windows and the storm window.

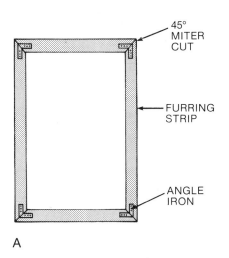

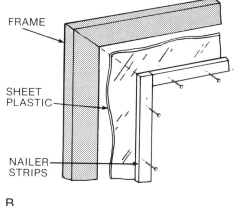

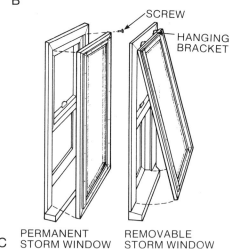

Fig. 14-1: (A) Use angle irons to secure window frame pieces. (B) Use nailer strips, tacked in place, to secure plastic to the frame. (C) Apply foam weatherstripping and screw the frame into place.

Blinds and Drapes

Blinds and drapes can be important energy-savers. In the winter, they can be closed at night to greatly reduce heat loss through windows. In the summer, they can be closed in the daytime—particularly when windows are exposed to direct sunlight—to reduce the load on the air conditioner.

Some kinds of blinds and drapes are more energy-efficient than others. Look for blinds that have a tight seal around all edges, and blinds and drapes that are made of insulating materials.

Blocking Solar Heat Gain

Winter heat loss is not the only reason that windows should be weather-proofed. Radiated heat gain through the windows during the summer cooling season accounts for much of the cost of air-conditioning a home. The radiant heat gain through windows alone for a typical home on an average summer day accounts for one-third of the total cooling load. Table 14-1 compares the solar heat screening ability of a number of window treatments. The figures contained in the table are only approximate. They represent maximum summer conditions and will be lower in winter.

Table 14-1: Solar Screening Ability of Various Materials

Material	Heat Gain Reduction
Standard glass	0
Draperies (depending on fabric & color)	45% to 60%
Venetian blinds	25%
Thermal glass	40%
Tinted glass	48%
Double-glazed glass	60%
Triple-glazed glass	70%
Reflective film:	
silver & gold	75%
bronze	60%
smoke	50%
Fiberglass screen	68%
Canvas awning	75%
Light tree shading	45%
Dense tree shading	80%
Overhanging roof	80%
Aluminum louvered screening	80% to 86%

Note: Figures are approximate and represent maximum summer conditions. Figures are lower in winter.

VESTIBULES

A vestibule, closed breezeway, or other "air-lock" type entryway between the outdoors and a main door leading into the heated area of your home will reduce infiltration and air changes when you go in and out. Be sure to enter and leave your home through this entryway during peak heating and cooling months.

USING ENERGY EFFICIENTLY

Most, if not all, American homes are dependent on electricity. We use electricity to cook our food, to dry our clothes, to brush our teeth, to provide our entertainment (radio, television, etc.), to churn our ice cream, to carve our turkey, and to do a multitude of other things. Many households use it to heat their water and to heat and cool their homes. Figure 14-2 shows how the average all-electric home in a 3,500 annual degree-day area uses electricity. The percentages shown describe a 1,500 square foot house with R-19 insulation in the attic, R-11 in the walls, and R-7 under the floor, plus storm windows and storm doors. The use of electricity in your home will certainly vary from these percentages according to your climate, heating system, and personal life-style. For example, a home in Miami, Florida, will spend more for air-conditioning than a similar home in Bangor, Maine, which may use no air-conditioning at all. Yet, while the percentages may vary, heating units, air conditioners, water heaters, refrigerator/ freezers, ranges, and clothes dryers will be the largest end-users of electricity in any household. By carefully monitoring the use of these appliances, you can reduce energy consumption in your home. For example, water-saving devices, such as "low flow" showerheads and sink aerators, can reduce your hot water use significantly. In particular, a water-saving showerhead can greatly reduce your hot water use—while still providing a satisfying shower. An efficient showerhead can pay for itself in a matter of weeks.

Energy-efficient appliances for kitchen and laundry can save you money. Check to see if the refrigerator, washer, dryer, and water heater are labeled or sold as "energy-efficient." The savings from these particular energy-efficient appliances justifies their slightly higher cost.

Fluorescent lights should be installed instead of incandescent (light bulb) lights wherever practical—for example, in the kitchen, bathrooms, laundry, and work spaces. They use about a fourth of the power used by ordinary incandescent lights.

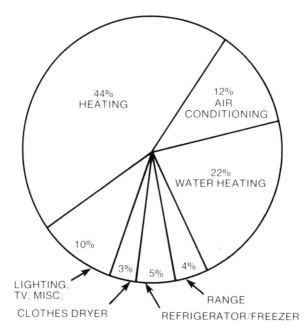

Fig. 14-2: Energy consumption in a 1,500 square foot house in a 3,500 DD area.

IMPROVING A HEATING SYSTEM

Insulating, caulking, weatherstripping, and landscaping will increase the energy efficiency of any home. But if your heating system is inefficient, the heating/cooling costs of maintaining a comfortable home environment will remain excessive. As previously explained, most of the Btu contained in fossil fuels such as oil, gas, and coal are lost via the smokestack, operating jacket, and off-cycle of a heating unit. The average heating system wastes 25% to 50% of the potential Btu capacity of the fuel.

Improving the seasonal efficiency of a heating system can save a substantial amount in heating expenses. Table 14-2 lists the savings per $100 of annual fuel costs that can result by increasing the efficiency of your heating system. There are several reasons why your heating system may not be functioning at top efficiency. Have a qualified serviceman service your heat system before every heating season, and ask for suggestions on how you can improve the system's efficiency. For example, there are devices available that can reduce flue gas heat losses when the furnace is not operating, recover heat from stack gas before it enters the chimney, and lower boiler water temperatures when the outside temperature is mild. Your oil or gas company can help you determine whether these energy efficiency devices can be used in your heating system, as well as the expected fuel savings.

Table 14-2: Dollar Savings per $100 of Annual Fuel Cost

From Original Efficiency of	To an Increased Efficiency of					
	55%	60%	65%	70%	75%	80%
50%	$9.10	$16.70	$23.10	$28.60	$33.00	$37.50
55%		8.30	15.40	21.50	26.70	31.20
60%			7.70	14.30	20.00	25.00
65%				7.10	13.30	18.80
70%					6.70	12.50
75%						6.30

Fireplaces and Wood Stoves

Fireplaces and wood stoves used in conjunction with standard heating systems can sometimes offer significant energy savings (if firewood can be obtained inexpensively), *but only if the unit is of closed combustion design with an outside combustion air intake.* "Closed combustion design" means that the wood is burned in an enclosed space that is not directly exposed to the room. In the case of a fireplace, this means that it will have a closed glass front along with an outside combustion air intake. An "outside combustion air intake" allows the fireplace or stove to draw cold air from outdoors instead of heated air from indoors. Ordinary stoves and fireplaces are inefficient because they draw large amounts of heated indoor air up the chimney.

Uninsulated Ducts and Pipes

One easy way for you to get more heat from your heating system is to insulate the pipes and ductwork. In most central heating systems, hot air, water, or steam is forced through a network of ducts and pipes. These often originate or pass through unheated basements or crawl spaces. If the pipes and ducts are not insulated, heat will escape into the unheated areas where it will be wasted.

Ducts. The first step when insulating ducts is to extrude duct sealant into the joints of the sheet metal. Often the low-velocity systems installed in homes are not properly sealed where the duct sections meet. Hot air is forced out through the cracks and lost. Seal the joints with duct sealant, and eliminate this source of energy loss.

After the ducts are sealed, wrap them with 2" fiberglass batts with vapor barriers. Cut the batt to fit around the duct, wrap it around with the vapor barrier facing out, and tape the edges together. Be careful not to compress the insulation any more than necessary. As you wrap each batt around the duct, tape the batts together so that a continuous blanket is formed (Fig. 14-3). Any gap left between the batts will result in a heat leak.

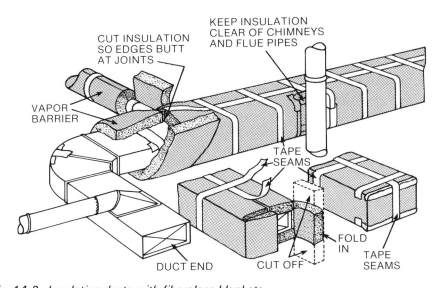

Fig. 14-3: Insulating ducts with fiberglass blankets.

In some situations, especially in low crawl spaces, the ducts will be difficult to reach and even harder to insulate. It may not be possible to wrap the insulation completely around the ducts after construction of a house is complete. If you find that to be the case, spray a pressure-sensitive adhesive (available in aerosol spray cans) on the duct to hold the insulation in place until it can be permanently affixed (Fig. 14-4).

Pipes. Hot water pipes should also be insulated. Foam tape is often used. Simply wrap the foam tape around the pipe, being careful not to leave gaps between the winds of the tape (Fig. 14-5A). The foam tube, though, is most common. The tubes are sized to fit a particular size of pipe and are slit so that the tube can be slipped over the pipe. Once installed, the slit must be taped shut (Fig. 14-5B). Batt insulation may also be cut to fit around pipes. Carefully tape all joints where insulating pieces meet.

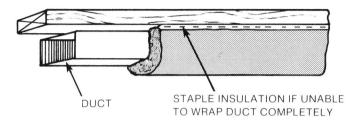

DUCT

STAPLE INSULATION IF UNABLE
TO WRAP DUCT COMPLETELY

Fig. 14-4: Insulating ducts in confined areas.

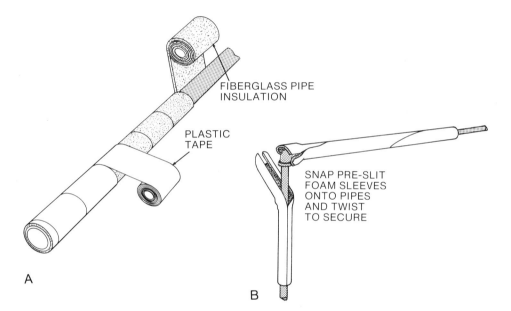

FIBERGLASS PIPE INSULATION

PLASTIC TAPE

SNAP PRE-SLIT FOAM SLEEVES ONTO PIPES AND TWIST TO SECURE

A

B

Fig. 14-5: Insulating pipes with (A) foam tape or (B) foam tubes.

Water-Heating Systems

The electric water heater is on duty 24 hours a day, 365 days a year so you can wash your dishes, your clothes, and yourself. The average family of four uses 65 gallons of water a day and twice the amount of energy needed to satisfy domestic hot water needs. This is why heating water averages 22% of your annual electric bill.

To reduce the energy consumed in heating water, insulate your water heater to reduce tank standby losses. Water heater insulation kits are available in all sizes and are easy to install. Improving your tank insulation is a particularly good energy conservation measure, especially for older water heaters. In some cases, it is possible to save 10% of your water-heating energy by adding the proper insulation.

Kits usually contain precut R-6 insulation of 1-1/2" thick fiberglass or 3/8" thick foam inside a vinyl or similar cover, plus tape to seal the joints. Kits for electric heaters cover both top and sides (Fig. 14-6A); those for gas heaters cover only sides (Fig. 14-6B). To install, all you need is a tape measure and a pair of scissors; mark and cut out holes to expose the controls and the drain valve. Wrap the insulating blanket around the heater and tape the joints and edges.

If you make a blanket for an electric heater, use R-6 or R-9 fiberglass batt insulation with a foil vapor barrier. Cut batt to lengths equal to the circumference of the tank; wrap lengths around the tank, beginning at the bottom. Cut holes to expose the controls as you go. Hold lengths temporarily in place with string or by spraying an aerosol adhesive onto the tank. After cutting a disc for the top, tape it to the top section; then tape all horizontal joints. Tape the vertical joint last after removing strings.

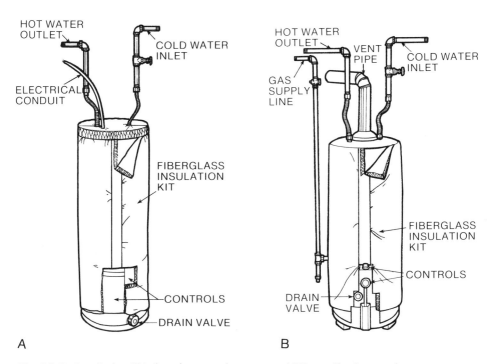

Fig. 14-6: Insulating (A) electric water heaters and (B) gas-fired water heaters.

EXHAUST FANS AND WHOLE-HOUSE FANS

Whole-house fans (Fig. 14-7) differ from power attic ventilators (which are similar in appearance to the passive attic ventilator shown in Fig. 10-19, but with a built-in fan unit) mainly in that they exhaust air from the *whole* house, not just the attic. Whole-house fans allow you to be comfortable, at many times of the year, without using air conditioning. But they can also be a major investment.

Exhaust fans are very desirable in air-conditioned homes in the kitchen, bathrooms, and laundry room. They should be used in the summer whenever

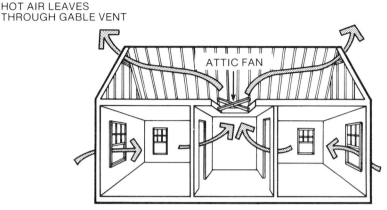

HOT AIR LEAVES
THROUGH GABLE VENT

ATTIC FAN

COOLER NIGHT AIR
REPLACES HOT AIR

Fig. 14-7: A whole-house fan.

moisture is being produced by cooking, showers, or laundry. In order to effective-ly cool a home, an air conditioner must remove moisture from the air. Excessive moisture in the home increases the amount of work the air conditioner has to do—and increases the cost of running it. Some new homes are built so tightly that moisture must be exhausted in both winter and summer to prevent moisture build-up and condensation problems indoors.

Exhaust fans should have dampers that automatically shut tightly when the fan is not running. The damper should be inspected periodically to make sure that it is working properly. This is particularly important for roof-mounted dampers, which tend to become clogged with leaves. Clothes dryers should always be directly vented to the outdoors.

Other Cooling Systems Tips

Averaging a little over 12% of your total annual bill, air-conditioning is the third largest user of electricity in your home. To save money while staying cool, you should:

● Clean or change cooling equipment filters frequently—preferably once a month.

● Keep all cooling equipment in good working condition.

● Remove trapped dirt and dust from cooling grills or outlets.

● Make certain that furniture and draperies do not block cooling outlets. This can restrict air circulation, overwork the cooling equipment, and increase operat-ing costs.

● During the summer, try to restrict the use of heat-producing appliances to the cooler hours of the morning or evening. Additional heat from appliances will place additional burden on air-conditioning equipment.

● Keep storm doors and windows in place to reduce the air-conditioning load. Keep outside doors and windows closed.

● For maximum economy, it is recommended that thermostats be set at 78° to 80°F during the summer. Lower temperature settings may improve comfort; however, circulating cooled air may permit a higher temperature setting.

● Check closely for ductwork leaks, especially at connection points. Repair leaks with duct tape or an acrylic latex caulk. Insulate ducts installed in such unconditioned spaces as attics, vented crawl spaces, garages, and basements (Fig. 14-8).

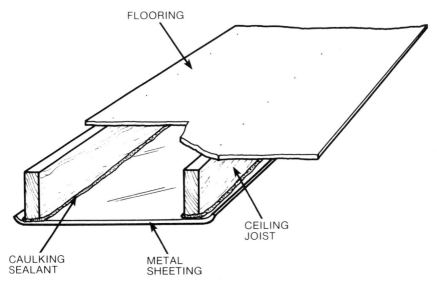

Fig. 14-8: Caulking around ceiling joist and metal sheeting to insulate ductwork.

Glossary

Abrasion resistance. Resistance of a substance to wear caused by mechanical action on a surface of the substance.

Accelerated aging. Short term laboratory simulation of normal long-term aging processes. Experiments to simulate aging include controls of temperature, light, oxygen, water, and other significant aging factors. In recent years, the adhesives industry has come to rely more and more on the "oxygen bomb" test as an indicator of the relative life expectancy of a given formulation.

Accelerated weathering. Laboratory simulation of the worst effects of long-term natural weathering. Adhesives are generally not subjected, in most household applications, to the severe conditions that are simulated in many weathering tests of adhesives.

Accelerator. An ingredient used in small amounts to speed up the action of a hardener.

Acrylic latex. A generic term for synthetic rubbers obtained by polymerization from acrylic and methylacrylic acids. Other acrylic polymers include lightweight plastics and resins. Acrylic latex polymers are used chiefly in paints and adhesives.

Adhere. To stick to the surface of another object; hold two or more objects together by clinging to their surfaces.

Adherend. A body that is joined to another body by an adhesive substance.

Adhesion. The property of surface attachment, or sticking to a surface. The adhesion of a caulk is its property of sticking to a substrate.

Adhesive, cold-setting. An adhesive that sets at temperatures below 68°F (20°C).

Adhesive, contact. An adhesive that is apparently dry, but develops the property of adhesion instantaneously upon application of pressure. Contact adhesives are also called contact bond adhesives and dry bond adhesives.

Adhesive, dispersion. A system, or mixture, in which an adhesive substance is suspended, or dispersed, in a liquid.

Adhesive, failure. Rupture at the adhesive-adherend interface—the separation of the adhesive from the adherend.

Adhesive, foamed. An adhesive through which many small gas-filled cells are dispersed. Foamed adhesive is also called cellular adhesive.

Adhesive, heat activated. A dry adhesive film that is rendered tacky or fluid by the application of heat, or both heat and pressure, to the assembly.

Adhesive, hot melt. An adhesive that is applied in a liquid, heated state, and forms a bond as it cools and solidifies.

Adhesive, hot-setting. An adhesive that requires a temperature at or above 100°C (212°F) to set.

Adhesive, intermediate temperature setting. An adhesive that sets in the temperature range of 31° to 99°C (87° to 211°F).

Adhesive, multiple layer. An adhesive film carrying two different adhesives, one on each side, that is designed to bond an assembly of dissimilar materials, such as the core-to-face bond of a sandwich composite.

Adhesive, pressure-sensitive. A viscoelastic material that remains permanently tacky. Pressure-sensitive adhesives adhere instantaneously to most solid surfaces with the application of very slight pressure.

Adhesive, room temperature setting. An adhesive that sets in the temperature range of 20° to 30°C (68° to 86°F).

Adhesive, separate application. A term used to denote a dual adhesive treatment consisting of the application of one adhesive material to one adherend and the other to the other adherend, after which the two adherends are brought together to form a joint.

Adhesive, solvent. An adhesive having a volatile organic liquid as a vehicle.

Adsorption. The assimilation, or taking up, of gases or liquids by the surface layer of a solid object or body of liquid.

Aging. Normal progressive deterioration of the original chemical and physical properties of an object or substance.

Air changes per hour (ACH). The number of replacements of the entire volume of conditioned air inside a building by an equal volume of outside air during one hour. Such air changes occur primarily through the processes of exfiltration and infiltration.

Alligatoring. Cracking of a surface into segments so that it resembles the hide of an alligator.

Ambient temperature. The surrounding temperature—the temperature of an environment. The temperature of the air surrounding an object is its ambient temperature.

Anaerobic. The characteristic of being viable in the absence of oxygen. Adhesives that cure in the absence of oxygen are described as anaerobic.

Annual degree-days. The total of all the degree-days occurring in a given location during its heating season. The higher the number of annual degree-days, the harsher the heating season.

Assembly. A term used here to denote a group of adherends, with their adhesive material, that have been placed together for bonding or bonded together.

Asphalt. A naturally occurring bituminous pitch, normally brown to black in color. Asphalt-based adhesives have a tendency to bleed through paint, but are sometimes used to mount gypsum drywall.

Batch. A manufactured unit or a collection of two or more manufactured units of the same kind.

Band joist. An upright 2 by 8 or 2 by 10 joist that rests on the sole plate of a wall. Wall insulation should always cover the band joist.

Batt insulation. Pieces of glass fiber or rock wool insulation, 16" or 24" wide and 4' or 8' long.

Bead. A term used here to denote a continuous application of an adhesive or sealant material, in the form of a strip or ribbon. Other forms of application are discontinuous, such as spots and globs.

Beadboard. A polystyrene insulation material with a very fine pore structure.

Binder. A term used here to denote a component of a mixture that provides the property of adhesion.

Blanket insulation. Long rolls of glass fiber or rock wool insulation.

Blister. A term used here to denote a small bump on the surface of an adherend. The boundaries of a blister may be irregular and its face may be concave or flattened.

Blown-in insulation. Loose insulation injected into a wall cavity or attic by means of a special machine.

Bond. A term used here to denote both the actual region of attachment, and the state of attachment, of an adhesive application with its adherends.

Bond face. The part or surface of an adherend that serves as a substrate for an adhesive.

Bond strength. The amount of tension, compression, flexure, peel, impact, cleavage, shear, or any other mechanical force, that is required to separate an adhesive assembly along or nearly along the plane of the bond.

British thermal unit. One Btu is defined as the amount of heat necessary to raise one pound of water 1°F. British thermal units are used to express the amount of energy used in heating.

Butadiene styrene sealant. A caulk containing SBR rubber. SBR rubber caulks are adhesive and very resistant to ultraviolet, but do not form effective barriers to water.

Butyl rubber caulks. Caulks containing butyl rubber, a synthetic rubber obtained by polymerization. Butyl rubber caulks display excellent sealing qualities, including water resistance, making them suitable for use in gutters and downspouts, and on driveways, concrete blocks, and other areas that are frequently exposed to moisture (but not to continuous immersion).

Capping. A term used here to denote insulation that is placed in the ceilings and roof structure of a building to create a thermal cap. Capping reduces the conduction of heat that is transferred to the ceiling areas by convection.

Catalyst. A substance that is combined in small quantities with another substance or mixture in order to initiate or promote a chemical reaction.

Caulking. A flexible material used to fill gaps where two different surfaces of the house meet.

Cellular material. A solid substance through which many small cells are dispersed. The cells contained in such a material may be both open and closed and may contain air or various gases

Checking. A term used here to denote the development of slight breaks or cracks in the surface of a caulk or adhesive.

Circuit. An assembly of electrical or electronic elements that forms the complete path of an electrical current.

Clear sealant. A semi-transparent caulk with adhesion, permanent flexibility, and high resistance to moisture, light, and other destructive factors and conditions. Clear sealants include silicone caulks, which normally are clear and remain clear, and some butadiene styrene and acrylic caulks.

Climatic setting. The temperatures, humidity, sunlight, wind, and other meteorological phenomena that are normally experienced in a particular place over a year, or other specified long period of time.

Clock thermostat. A thermostat that automatically raises and lowers the indoor temperature at specified times of the day or night.

Coefficient of expansion. A mathematical expression of the ratio of the amount of linear expansion, or change in length, of an object, for every degree (Celsius) of temperature increase above 0°C.

Coefficient of performance. A measure of the efficiency of a heat pump or air conditioner. The COP is defined as the number of Btu's of heat that are moved between indoors and outdoors by each Btu of input energy used to operate the unit. A unit with a higher COP is more efficient. The COP is proportional to the EER.

Cohesion. The state of attraction between the molecules or other particles of a given body, in which the particles stick together, and remain unified, throughout the mass of the body.

Cohesive failure. Failure of an adhesive characterized by tearing apart, or internal division, of the mass of the adhesive itself.

Cohesive strength. A term used to denote the maximum force under which a body of adhesive is able to remain unified under stress. Cohesive strength is expressed in psi.

Collar beams. Beams that connect the rafters of both sides of a gable-roofed structure, and on which attic ceilings may be suspended.

Condensation. The reduction of a vapor of a liquid (such as water vapor), or a gas (such as steam), to a denser state as a body of liquid. The condensation of water vapor that enters tightly enclosed areas of a building, such as the wall cavities, can become a serious problem unless there is adequate ventilation to evaporate the water as it condenses—or unless the entry of water vapor is reduced or prevented.

Conduction. Transfer of heat that occurs directly from warmer molecules to cooler ones. Conduction does not involve the movement of matter from one place to another. It is the primary mode of heat flow in a house.

Consistency. A term used here to denote that property of a liquid adhesive which is its resistance to physical deformation after it has set and solidified.

Convection. The transfer of heat by the movement of molecules of gaseous and liquid substances from one place to another.

Convective air currents. Drafts consisting of warm air molecules moving and transferring heat to cold surfaces such as windows, and the resulting chilled air molecules moving down to take the place of the remaining warm air molecules that are still travelling toward the cold surfaces.

Cost-effectiveness. A measure of the degree to which an energy-efficiency measure results in savings that pay for its original purchase cost. A measure with high cost-effectiveness, other things being equal, is a better investment than one with low cost-effectiveness.

Crazing. Fine cracks that may extend in a network on, or through, or under the surface of an application of adhesive.

Creep. Deformation over a period of time of a solid body under constant load. Creep is also called cold flow.

Cross bracing. Rafter supporting members of the roof of a building. Cross braces must be insulated to keep the attic free of heat leaks, and should not be overlooked when unfinished attics are being insulated.

Cure. A term used here to denote the process of hardening, or setting, of an adhesive. Adhesive cures may involve physical processes, such as evaporation, and various chemical reactions.

Cure time. The time required to effect a complete cure at a given temperature.

Curing agent. A term used here to denote a chemical which is added to effect a cure in a polymer. A curing agent is also called a hardener.

Degree day. A measure of winter climate severity: One degree day is 1°F difference between the average outdoor temperature for the day and a standard temperature of 65°F. Yearly heating costs are roughly proportional to annual degree days.

Dry. To lose free solvent constituents or other liquids through such physical processes as evaporation and absorption, or by chemical change. The drying of an adhesive, the loss of its solvents, may involve significant changes in its physical properties and appearance of the adhesive substance itself.

Elasticity. The property of a solid or semisolid object that reassumes its original shape after removal of a load.

Electric furnace. A centrally-located device which heats air with electric resistance heating elements for distribution throughout the house.

Electric resistance heat. Heat produced by the flow of electricity through high-resistance wire, tape, or film.

Elongation recovery. A term used here to denote the property of returning to full size, or regaining original length, after a period of compression.

Emulsion. A mixture of two incompletely miscible liquids, or a semi-permanent suspension of fine particles in water or some other aqueous liquid.

Emulsion-based adhesives. Adhesive mixtures containing water as their main, or only, solvent constituent.

Emulsion systems. Combinations of incompatible or incompletely miscible liquids, in which small globules of one liquid are evenly dispersed throughout another liquid substance.

End walls. The walls that form the ends of an attic or similar enclosure in a gable-roofed or other slope-roofed building. An end wall narrows or comes to a point at the top, following the diagonal lines of the rafters.

Energy audit. A detailed inspection of a building to determine its energy efficiency. An energy audit involves the identification of any inadequately insulated areas, and the discovery of any sources of infiltrating air.

Energy efficiency ratio. A measure of air conditioner efficiency. The EER is defined as the number of Btu's of heat removed from the house by an air conditioner per watt of electrical energy used to operate the unit. A unit with a higher EER is more efficient.

Epoxies. Tough, hard synthetic resins obtained by polymerization, and noted for their excellent adhesive properties.

Exfiltration. The escape of warm air from a house. Exfiltration stimulates infiltration by causing a drop in air pressure inside the house.

Extender. A term used here to denote any material that is used to increase the volume and lower the cost of an adhesive.

Extruded polystyrene board. Rigid polystyrene board insulation, normally white or blue in color. Polystyrene has the highest thermal resistance of any available insulation material, but is flammable and not compatible with many adhesive solvents.

Extrusion. A term used here to denote the application of a semisolid adhesive or sealant by pressing-out or squeezing the material from its container (such as a caulking gun) onto the substrate surface, or into cracks.

Fatigue failure. Failure of a material through rapid cyclic deformation, such as alternating periods of compression and release, or cyclic stretching or twisting.

Filler. Finely ground material that is added to extend an adhesive, or to change or improve certain properties.

Flow. A term used here to denote any movement of an adhesive during the bonding process before the adhesive is set.

Foamed-in-place insulation. Insulation materials, such as urethane, that are blown or sprayed in place as liquid foams, which subsequently harden. Foamed-in-place insulation is suitable for application in otherwise inaccessible areas, such as the cavities in finished walls.

Forced convection. A convection current that is accelerated or modified by mechanical means. A fan that blows heated air down to the cool floor area in a building creates a forced convection current.

Gel. A semisolid dispersive system consisting of a very fine aggregate of one or more solid substances held in close association with a liquid substance or solution.

Glue. A term that today is almost synonymous with the term "adhesive". But for centuries, glue was known only as a hard gelatin extracted from hides, tendons, cartilage, bones, and other animal sources. This animal-derived glue was prepared for use by heating in water. Other glues, or adhesives, have since been developed from petroleum and other non-animal sources.

Green strength. The relative cohesive strength of an adhesive, glue, or mastic in the wet state. Green strength is also called tack, initial tack, and green grab.

Hardener. A substance or mixture of substances used to promote or control a curing reaction. Such a substance is often added to control the degree of hardness of the cured adhesive. Hardeners are also called curing agents.

Heat. A form energy associated with the random movement of molecules, atoms, and even smaller units of matter. Unlike temperature, which is a measure of the level or concentration of heat in an object, a measurement of heat energy, as such, is a measurement of the amount of this energy contained in a given body.

Heat flow. The transfer of thermal energy from an area of warm temperature to an area of cool temperature.

Infiltration. Convective flow of cool air into a house that is associated with the escape of warm air (exfiltration), and accelerated by the development of lower air pressure inside than outside the house.

Inhibitor. A term used here to denote a substance that delays or prevents a chemical reaction. Inhibitors are sometimes used in certain types of adhesives to prolong storage or working life. An inhibitor may also be called a retarder.

Insulating glass. Two layers of glass with an air space in between, manufactured as a single unit.

Joint. A term used here to denote the location at which two adherends are held together with a layer of adhesive.

Joint, lap. A joint made by placing one adherend partly over another and bonding together the overlapped portions.

Joint, starved. A joint that has an insufficient amount of adhesive to produce a satisfactory bond.

Joists. The beams that support a floor or ceiling.

Knee walls. The low walls that form the sides of an attic or similar enclosure in a gable-roofed building (or one side of such an enclosure in a shed-roofed building). The top line of a knee wall is the line along which the rafters meet the upright framing members of the building.

Latex caulks. Caulks containing synthetic latex that is obtained by polymerization. These caulks require protection from sunlight, but under proper conditions are effective sealants.

Loose-fill. Insulation in aggregate form. Loose-fill insulation materials, including styrofoam, vermiculite, and perlite, can be poured into areas that cannot be reached to install boards or hang batts.

Metal framing adhesives. Neoprene-based adhesives that are suitable for bonding wood, gypsum board, and other building materials to metal framing members and surfaces. Metal framing adhesives have high initial tack, bond over a wide range of temperatures, and are flammable.

Mean radiant temperature. The temperature of surrounding surfaces. By insulating walls, floors, ceilings, and windows, the mean radiant temperature of a building can be raised, making it more comfortable.

Natural convection. A convection current that is not assisted by mechanical means.

Neoprene. The synthetic rubber that is obtained by polymerization from chloroprene. Neoprene is characterized by resistance to oils, ultraviolet light, ozone, and other factors and conditions that destroy other rubbers.

Oil-based caulk. Caulk consisting usually of oil and a clay filler. Oil-based caulks have been used for centuries but are inferior in most respects (except initial cost) to the modern elastomeric caulks. Oil-based caulks are most useful in interior applications where they are not subjected to joint movement, ultraviolet light, moisture, temperature extremes, etc.

Oxidation. Any chemical reaction in which oxygen atoms join another substance, resulting in a new chemical that contains oxygen (or more oxygen). Oxygen, especially in the form of ozone, causes deterioration of many rubbery materials.

Penetration. A term used here to denote the absorption or adsorption of an adhesive into an adherend.

Permanence. A term used to denote the degree of resistance of an adhesive bond to deteriorating factors.

Phenolics. Synthetic varnish resins made from phenol and an aldehyde (such as formaldehyde).

Plasticity. The property of remaining unified, holding together without rupture, in spite of cyclic or permanent deformation.

Polyesters. Complex esters obtained by polymerization. Polyesters are used resins, as fibers, and as a raw material for the manufacture of other plastics.

Polymer. Any compound formed by a process of polymerization.

Polyvinyl acetate. A synthetic resin obtained by polymerization from vinyl acetate. Polyvinyl acetate (PVA) latex caulks are usually superior to oil-based caulks, but will disintegrate when used in exterior applications where they are in contact with cement.

Primer. A term used here to denote a coating applied to a surface, prior to the application of an adhesive, in order to improve the performance of the bond.

R-value. A mathematical expression of the time (measured in hours, or fractions of hours) per Btu of heat transmission through a section of a material or composite of materials that is one square foot in area and of any given thickness, when there is a difference of $1\,°F$ between the ambient temperatures of each opposite one square foot surface of the section. R-values are measures of thermal resistance.

Radiation. Transfer of energy in the form of heat rays or waves. Unlike conduction or convection, radiation occurs in all directions simultaneously and does not require contact by any conducting material.

Rafters. A series of structural roof members spanning from an exterior wall to the center beam or ridge board of a roof.

Resin. One of many solid or semisolid, amorphous, fusible, and flammable, complex organic materials, such as the naturally occurring copals, dammars, amber and mastics, and the many synthetic resins, including the acrylic and phenolic resins. Resins soften or melt easily, and they tend to flow when subjected to stress. Many resins have plastic properties, and may also be classified as plastics. On the other hand, many plastic materials have the properties of resins.

Retrofit. Alteration of a home or addition of materials or devices to improve its energy performance.

Ridge vent. A vent located along the ridge, or at the highest point of a sloping roof. The ridge vent forms, along with the soffit vents, an escape route for moisture that would otherwise accumulate inside the roof structure and between the other structural members of a building.

Rosin. A resin obtained from the sap of the pine tree (gum rosin), or by extraction from the wood itself (wood rosin).

Rubber-based caulks. Premium-grade caulks consisting primarily of rubbers, rather than acrylics, acetates, butyls, butadiene styrene, and silicones. Rubber-based caulks have long life expectancy, and are suitable for most applications.

Set. A term used here to denote the fixing or hardening of an adhesive, whether by polymerization, oxidation, vulcanization, gelation, hydration, or evaporation, or any other process.

Shrinkage. The percentage of weight lost by an adhesive during set, under specified conditions.

Silicone caulk. Any caulk containing silicone. Silicone caulks are adhesive, flexible, resilient, and resistant to chemicals and ultraviolet—over a very wide temperature range.

Silicone rubber. A synthetic rubber obtained by polymerization from organic compounds (siloxanes) that contain the element silicon.

Sill plate. The horizontal board, lying flat on top of the foundation, on which the outer wall rests.

Sill sealing insulation. Insulation placed between foundation and sill to prevent air leakage.

Sizing. A term used here to denote the process of applying a material on a surface to fill pores and reduce the absorption of any subsequently-applied coating. Sizing, which is done before applying adhesive, can modify other surface properties of the substrate to improve the bond. Material applied in a sizing operation is called a size.

Slippage. The movement of adherends with respect to each other during the bonding process.

Soffit vents. Vents present on the underside of a part or member of a building.

Solvent. Any liquid in which another substance can be dissolved.

Solvent-based adhesives. Adhesive mixtures of which the sole or primary solvent constituent is not water.

Spindle Anchors. Long pins with perforated flat bases (by which they are attached to framing members) on which batt insulation is impaled.

Spread. A term used here to denote the quantity of adhesive applied per unit of joint area. Spread is usually expressed in points of adhesive per thousand square feet. "Single spread" denotes an application of adhesive to only one adherend of a joint. "Double spread" denotes an application of adhesive to both adherends of a joint.

Squeeze out. A term used here to denote the mass of adhesive that squeezes out of an assembly at the bond line when pressure is applied to the adherends.

Storage life. The period of time during which a product can be stored under specified temperature conditions and still remain suitable for use. Storage life is also called shelf life.

Strapping. A term that is used here to denote flexible, thin, flat strips of metal that can be fastened around batt insulation, to hold it in place.

Strength, dry. A term used here to denote the strength of an adhesive joint immediately after drying under specified conditions or after a period of conditioning in the laboratory.

Strength, wet. A term used here to denote the strength of an adhesive joint immediately after removal from a liquid in which it has been immersed, under specified conditions of time, temperature, and pressure.

Stress. Force per unit of area, usually expressed in pounds per square inch (psi).

Structural adhesive. A bonding agent used for transferring required loads between adherends exposed to service environments that are typical for the structure involved.

Substrate. A term used here to denote the surface of any material on which an adhesive-containing substance is spread for any purpose, whether for bonding or simply as a coating.

Tack. The formation of a bond of measurable strength immediately after adhesive and adherend are brought into contact under low pressure.

Tack-free time. The amount of time it takes for the surface of a sticky material to skin over. A short tack-free time is a valuable characteristic, since dust and dirt are given little opportunity to collect on the surface of the material.

Tackiness. Stickiness.

Tear strength. The load required to tear apart a sealant specimen.

Teeth. A term used here to denote projections or other surface irregularities formed by the breaking of the filaments or strings that may form when two adhesive-coated substrates are separated.

Temperature. The measure of the level or concentration of heat in an area or substance.

Temperature, curing. The temperature required by an adhesive or an assembly in order for the adhesive to cure.

Temperature, drying. The temperature required for the setting of an adhesive assembly, or adhesive in an assembly, or on an adherend.

Temperature, maturing. A temperature that is required to produce desired characteristics in bonded components.

Temperature, setting. The temperature to which an adhesive or an assembly is subjected to set the adhesive.

Tensile strength. Resistance of a material to a tensile (stretching) force.

Thermal break. A layer of insulating material between the inner and outer frames of a metal-framed window.

Thermal cap. An energy-conserving effect produced in a building by insulating ceilings, and especially the roof structure, to reduce conduction of the heat that rises to the ceiling areas.

Thermal energy. Heat energy, a form of energy associated with the random motion of molecules. The greater the thermal energy (heat) contained in an object, the greater the amount of molecular movement in that object.

Thermal mass. An expression used here to denote the ability of a solid object, or of a body of a non-solid substance, to absorb, store, and release a large amount of heat energy. The thermal masses of equal volumes of different substances vary with their density: Dense, heavy materials like concrete contain much more matter per unit of volume than light, thin substances such as air, or plastic foam. Since heat energy consists of the random movement of small bits of matter (atoms and molecules), the denser the substance (the more matter there is, and hence, the more small bits of matter there are per unit of volume), the more heat energy can be absorbed, stored, and released by that substance.

Thermal resistance. Resistance by a material to the conduction of heat. The thermal resistance of an object is normally expressed as an R-value. The higher the R-value of a material, the greater is its insulating effect.

Thermal shock. A large and rapid change of temperature that has deleterious effects upon the physical objects or living organisms subjected to the change.

Thermal short. A significant route of escape for heat energy by conduction.

Thermographic equipment. Equipment that can be used, at considerable expense, to make precise scientific measurements of the patterns and extent of conduction and convection in a building.

Thinner. A volatile liquid added to dilute another material or otherwise modify its consistency or other properties.

Thixotropic sealant. A sealant that will not slip or sag, and maintains its shape without sagging during the curing process. A thixotropic sealant can therefore be used in a joint in a vertical wall.

Time, curing. A term used to denote the period of time during which an adhesive assembly is subjected to heat or pressure, or both, in order to cure the adhesive.

Time, drying. A term used to denote the period of time during which an assembly or an adhesive on an adherend is allowed to dry, with or without the application of heat or pressure, or both.

Time, joint conditioning. The time interval between the removal of a joint assembly from the conditions of heat or pressure, or both, and the attainment of maximum bond strength. Joint conditioning time is sometimes called joint aging time.

Time, setting. The period of time during which an assembly is subjected to heat or pressure, or both, in order to set the adhesive.

Total cure time. The amount of time that is required for an adhesive or sealant to cure completely.

Toxic. Poisonous to a living organism. A toxic substance may be harmful or fatal if ingested, inhaled, or allowed to touch skin, eyes, or mucous membranes. Toxic components of adhesives and insulating materials include toluene, hexane, and acetone solvents, and refrigerant gases.

U-value. A mathematical expression of the amount of heat, measured in Btu, that is conducted during each hour (or one hour) through a section of a material (or composite of materials), of any depth or thickness, that is one square foot in area—when there is a difference of 1 °F in the ambient temperatures of the two opposite square foot surfaces of the section. U-values are measures of heat transmission, whereas R-values are measures of resistance to heat transmission.

Ultraviolet light. A short invisible wavelength of light, longer than X-rays but shorter than visible light. Most ultraviolet rays are produced by the sun, and have many deleterious effects, including deterioration of many rubbery materials.

Vapor barrier. A thin sheet of plastic or specially treated paper that resists penetration by moisture. Such a layer should normally be located on the side of a layer of insulation facing the interior of the house.

Vehicle. A term used here to denote the liquid component of an adhesive.

Viscosity. The ratio of the shear stress existing between laminae of moving fluid and the rate of shear between these laminae. Viscous fluids are thick and have slightly adhesive properties.

Weatherstripping. Flexible metal, vinyl, foam or felt material for preventing air leaks around the moving parts of windows and doors.

Webbing. Filaments or threads that may form when adhesive transfer surfaces are separated.

Working life. The period of time during which an adhesive, after mixing with catalyst, solvent, or other compounding ingredients, remains suitable for use. Working life is also called pot life.

Index

Adhesives, 1, 4-5, 31-44
  advantages of, 1
  history of, 4-5
  how to apply, 42-43
  how to select, 31-35
  types, 36-41, 43-44
    ceiling tile, 41
    flooring, 43-44
    foam board, 38
    gypsum drywall, 39
    metal framing and structural, 36-37
    panel, 37
    tileboard and wallboard, 40-41
Air-conditioning, energy-saving tips, 153-154, 159-160
Astragal weatherstripping, 77
Attics, 103-114
  insulating finished, 109-114
  insulating unfinished, 105-108
  safety precautions, 104-105
    repairing roof leaks and wiring, 104-105
    sealing the floor, 105

Baseboards, caulking, 67
Basement, insulating, 135-144
Bathroom, caulking, 69
British thermal unit (BTU), 12

Cartridge guns, 58, 60-62
  sizes, 58
  using, 60-62
Caulks and caulking, 45-53, 55-69
  advantages of, 45, 59
  baseboards, 67
  characteristics of, 50-51
  doors, 65
  how much to buy, 48
  how to apply, 60-64
  how to select, 45-47
  masonry and foundations, 66
  pipe and wire openings, 67
  siding junctions, 66
  sinks, 69
  sole plate, 68
  toilets, 69
  tub and shower, 69
  types, 48-53, 55-57
    acrylic latex, 52-53
    blacktop repair, 57
    butyl rubber, 49-50
    concrete patch, 57
    concrete repair, 57
    oil-based, 48-49
    polyvinyl acetate (PVA) latex, 52
    silicone, 55-56
    tub and tile, 57
  vents and exhaust fans, 68-69
  windows, 65
Ceiling tile adhesives, 41
Ceilings, 103, 115-118, 135-137
  advantages of insulating, 103, 115
  insulating cathedral, 115-118
  insulating the basement, 135-137

Door shoes, 77
Door sweeps, 76, 84
Doors, 65, 79, 82-85
  caulking, 65
  how to weatherstrip, 79, 82-85
    door sweeps, 84
    felt or foam strips, 79
    tension strips, 83
    threshold gaskets, 84-85
    tubular gaskets, 82
Drywall, 113-115
  how to install, 114-115
  in a finished attic, 113-114

Energy conservation, 1
Exfiltration (see Infiltration)

Foam board adhesives, 38
Foundations, 66, 135-144
  caulking, 66
  insulating crawl spaces, 139-142
  insulating exterior, 137-139
    with rigid board, 137-139
  insulating slab-on-grade, 143-144
  insulating unheated basement, 135-137

Garage doors, 85
Gaskets (see Weatherstripping)
Glazing compounds, 56, 70
  applying to windows, 70

Heat loss, 12-21
  calculating, 12-21
    for conduction, 16-17
    for convection, 18-20
    total, 20-21
Heat transfer, 8-11
Heating system, insulating, 155-158

ducts, 156
pipes, 156
water heater, 157-158
Humidity control, 2-3

Infiltration, 10, 28-30
definition of, 10
exterior areas, 29-30
interior areas, 29
testing for, 28-29
Insulation, 23-28, 91-101
advantages of, 91
attics, 103-114
batts or blankets, 95-96
calculating cost of, 101
ceilings, 103, 115-118
comparing types of, 92-93
foamed-in-place, 99-100
foundations, 135-144
how to select, 91-95
loose-fill, 97-98
cellulose fiber, 97-98
fiberglass, 97
perlite, 98
rock wool, 97
vermiculite, 98
measuring, 26-28
R-values, 23-25, 94
ASHRAE handbook, 94
minimum recommended, 23-25
reflective, 100-101
rigid board, 98-99
extruded polystyrene, 98-99
molded or expanded polystyrene, 99
polyisocyanurate, 99
polyurethane, 99
steel buildings, 145-150
walls, 119-134
Interlocking metal strips, 77-78

Magnetic weatherstripping, 77
Masonry, 66, 125-132, 134
caulking, 66
insulating walls, 125-132, 134
Metal building (see Steel buildings)
Metal furring, 134

Plywood paneling, 37, 120-123
adhesives, 37
applying to walls, 120-123

R-values, 12-15, 94
ASHRAE handbook, 94
of common building materials, 14-15
Rigid board insulation, 98-99, 112-114,
123-131, 134, 137-139, 147
foundations, 137-139
in the attic, 112-114
interior walls, 123-125
masonry walls, 125-131, 134
steel buildings, 146
types of, 98-99

Sealants, 1, 4-5, 45-47, 50-51, 53-54
advantages of, 1, 45
butadiene styrene (SBR), 53-54
characteristics of, 50-51
history of, 4-5
how to select, 45-47
Sinks, caulking, 69
Steel buildings, insulating, 145-150
advantages, 145
lightweight steel frame, 148-149
on-beam, 146-147
with fiberglass batts or blankets, 146
with rigid board, 147
using spindle anchors, 149-150
Storm windows, 151-152

Tension strips, 74-75
Toilets, caulking, 69
Tub and shower, caulking, 69

U-values, 13-15
of common building materials, 14-15

Ventilation considerations, 118

Walls, insulating, 119-134
finishing with plywood paneling, 120-123
interior, 119-120, 123-125
with batts or blankets, 119-120
with rigid board, 123-125
masonry, 125-134
exterior, 125-127
interior, with batts or blankets, 131-132
interior, with rigid board, 127-131
with metal strips, 134
Weatherstripping, 71-78
astragal, 77
comparison of, 72-73
door shoes, 77
door sweeps, 76
gaskets, 71, 74-76
bristle weatherstripping, 74
casement window, 75
felt strips, 71
foam strips, 74
threshold, 76
tubular, 74
interlocking metal strips, 77-78
magnetic, 77
tension strips, 74-75
Windows, 65, 70, 86-90, 151-153
awning, 89-90
casement, 89-90
double-hung, 86-88
how to caulk, 65
how to glaze, 70
how to weatherstrip, 86-88
compression gaskets, 88
tension strips, 86
tubular gaskets, 87
sliding, 86-88
solar screening materials, 153
storm, 151-152